AUSTRALIAN

QUILT
HERITAGE

MARGARET ROLFE

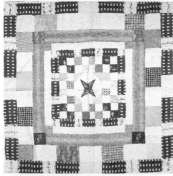

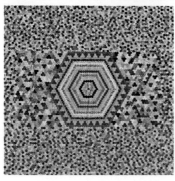

CONTENTS

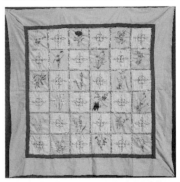
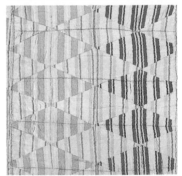
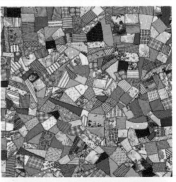

3

EDITORIAL
Managing Editor: Judy Poulos
Editorial Assistant: Ella Martin
Editorial Coordinator: Margaret Kelly
Editorial and Production Assistant: Heather Straton

PRODUCTION AND DESIGN
Production Director: Anna Maguire
Production Coordinator: Meredith Johnson
Production Editor: Sheridan Packer
Cover Design/Design Manager: Drew Buckmaster

PHOTOGRAPHERS
Mike Fisher, Andrew Sikorski, Andrew Payne, Bica Photographics,
Ken Stepnell, Michal Kluvanek, Steve Strike, Owen Hughes,
Brian Bolton, David Reid

Published by J.B. Fairfax Press Pty Limited
80-82 McLachlan Ave
Rushcutters Bay, Australia 2011
A.C.N. 003 738 430
Web: http://www.jbfp.com.au

Formatted by J.B. Fairfax Press Pty Limited

Printed by Toppan Printing Company, Singapore

JBFP 507

AUSTRALIAN QUILT HERITAGE
ISBN 1 86343 333 3

DISTRIBUTION AND SALES
Australia: J.B. Fairfax Press Pty Limited
Ph: (02) 9361 6366 Fax: (02) 9360 6262
USA: Quilters' Resource Inc.
2211 North Elston Ave
Chicago 60614
Ph: (773) 278 5695 Fax: (773) 278 1348

ACKNOWLEDGMENTS

While years of my life have gone into the research which underpins this book, it also could not have come into being without the assistance of many others.

I would like to thank all the people who generously allowed their quilts to be photographed: Bessie Bardwell, Wendy Benson, Lyn Brown, Belle Christie, Pearl Colefax, Dianne Gorringe, Jan Hall, Joyce Hedges, Judy Hooworth, Denise Lawler, Jack and Lurline Lydiard, Norma Meadley, Dr. E. Muirhead, Anne Semple, Wendy Springbett, Malcolm Staniforth, Jean Stuchbery, Joyce Walkely, Elizabeth Wallis, Fran Williams and Bev Wilmot.

I would like to acknowledge the immense contribution of my parents, Linda and Alex Poppins, for all their research on my behalf. Many people shared their research with me, and I thank Anne Bartlett, June Brown, Judy Crain, Dianne Finnegan, Wendy Hucker, Lyn Inall, Brenda Leitch and Alex Meldrum. Beryl and Alan Hodges made thoughtful criticisms of the text. John McPhee believed in what I was doing from the beginning and his support has been invaluable. I am grateful to Karen Fail and Judy Poulos of J.B. Fairfax Press who made this book happen. I thank all the photographers, but especially Mike Fisher, for their excellent photographs.

Throughout all stages of the book, from the earliest research to final proofreading, my husband, Barry, has always been there, encouraging, helping and keeping me focused. My debt to him is beyond words.

Margaret Rolfe

AUSTRALIAN
QUILT
HERITAGE

MARGARET ROLFE

INTRODUCTION

Quilts are important because they are one of the few tangible legacies that women leave. In the biblical words given by the American writer Eliza Calvert Hall to Aunt Jane of Kentucky, most women's work 'perishes with the usin'. The houses cleaned, the food cooked, the washing and ironing done, the dishes made shining, the gardens grown, and the clothing made and mended – all are work which disappears with time – often a matter of only minutes or hours. Nowadays, the value of women's work is further diminished as the word 'work' is reserved for what women do outside the home, dismissing all the efforts within the home of today's women, and almost all the efforts of women in the past. Yet, while it might not have been given a monetary value, such as the crop of wheat, the forged horseshoe or the well-made wheel which men produced, women's work underpinned existence, particularly in the past.

Food was often grown, and almost exclusively prepared, in the home. Keeping food cool was a problem in much of Australia, especially in summer. Cooking also necessitated keeping a fuel stove alight, no matter whether it was an icy cold winter morning or a searing hot summer midday. Clothes, especially children's clothes, underwear and nightwear, were sewn in the home, and warm tops, scarves and socks were knitted. Many toys were homemade. Tasks like washing and cleaning took days of physical work in the era before modern appliances, and often involved lighting fires and even carrying water. While chopping wood was considered a man's job, many a woman had to do it in the absence of a man or boy either capable or willing. Illness before modern drugs and immunisation meant lengthy convalescence in which women were the primary nurses. Babies were born at home, old people were cared for at home, and people died at home.

QUILT MADE BY MARTHA AND MARY RANDALL (top left) See page 15.
MEDALLION QUILT (left) See page 8.

Of all this work, little if anything remains. Today, processed and convenience foods, electrical appliances, clothing and bedding factories, nursery schools, hospitals, nursing homes, and last but not least, modern plumbing, replace most of the work that once women did in the home. But the quilts which women made do remain, giving us a window onto their lives.

Did most Australian women make quilts in the past? Perhaps not most, but certainly many, as shown by research that is continuing to uncover more and more quilts. Neither the overwhelming number of quilts which are found in the United States, nor the richness of the British quilt heritage, is found in Australia. Population size is an obvious factor and some quick comparisons make the point. In 1830, Australia had a population of seventy thousand, the United States had just under four million, and Britain had sixteen million. By 1900, Australia had a population of over three million, the United States had seventy-six million, and Britain had thirty-seven million. Climatic differences may have played a part, as in Australia there is no long confining winter in which outdoor activity is limited, a time that certainly many American women used to work on their quilts. Australia generally enjoys a temperate climate which may have made quiltmaking less essential than it was in colder climates. However, Australian winters are cold enough to require warm bedcovers, although this need was more usually met with woollen blankets rather than quilts.

The word 'quilt' was not universally used in the past; bedcovers which now would be called quilts were often called rugs. Australians, following the British practice, also used the word 'quilt' more loosely than Americans, as it could refer to a bedcover with one, two or three layers, and was not restricted to a three-layered sandwich of top, padding and backing that were quilted together. However, following the introduction of American quilting techniques after 1970, more use has been made of the word quilt, and American words for quiltmaking have become widespread. These words include 'to piece', meaning to seam two patches of fabric together, which in America is done with either a running stitch or by machine-stitching (in comparison with the oversewn pieced-over-papers style which Americans call 'English' or 'paper piecing'). A contrast is made between 'pieced' quilts, in which patches are sewn together, and 'appliqué' quilts, in which a patch of fabric is sewn onto a backing. Another introduced word is 'batting' instead of wadding, for the filling of a quilt.

Since first European settlement, Australia has been a nation of immigrants, and those immigrants brought quilts and quiltmaking skills with them. Before 1945, the immigrants predominantly came from the British Isles. Indeed, Australia was British, and saw itself an integral part of the Empire. Without either family proof of where a quilt was made or an obvious use of Australian motifs, it is impossible to tell whether an old quilt was made in Britain or Australia. Until well after the Second World War, styles of quiltmaking followed those found in the United Kingdom, which included Ireland for the greater part of this period. There is no identifiable style of quiltmaking

MIKE FISHER

which can be called indigenous to Australia. Rather, Australian women took existing styles to make their quilts, and some made individual variations and incorporated Australian motifs.

Prior to the 1970s, the major styles of quilts made in Australia were medallion quilts, pieced-over-papers patchwork, Log Cabin quilts, crazy patchwork, embroidered quilts, simply made utility quilts, Wagga rugs and Suffolk Puffs. There are some appliqué quilts, but relatively few.

The Medallion style of quiltmaking consists of taking a centre square, which may contain either pieced or appliqué work, or perhaps a printed motif, then surrounding it with successive patchwork borders to frame the centre. It is a style which is typical of early nineteenth century quilts, but the style continued in Australia throughout the century and into the next. The centre of the quilt is often the feature of the quilt, although sometimes the centre can be just a very simple shape.

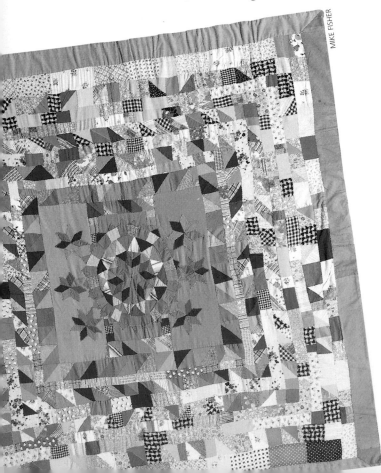

MIKE FISHER

MEDALLION QUILT (left), Tasmania, 1930s or 1940s. 198 cm x 206 cm (78 in x 81 in). Private collection.
DETAIL OF HEXAGONS PIECED OVER PAPERS (top). Made by the Country Women's Association members, Euroa, 1931. Collection of Euroa and District Historical Society.

BICA PHOTOGRAPHICS

BICA PHOTOGRAPHICS

From early times through until the present, a major style has been the pieced-over-papers patchwork, also sometimes called mosaic patchwork. In this method, shapes are precisely cut out of paper, a fabric patch is basted over the paper, then the prepared shapes are overstitched together. A template shape is used to make a pattern and scrap paper is cut into the shapes. In the past, children's exercise books were often the source of paper. The most common shapes were the hexagon, or diamonds deriving from the division of a hexagon, although other shapes such as squares and octagons were used. In the second half of the nineteenth century, these pieced quilts were often made of silk or combinations of silks and velvets, and diamonds put together to make a three-dimensional cube, the Baby Block pattern, was a particular favourite. The discovery of aniline dyes gave new bright colours such as royal purples, fuschias and bright greens. At this time, silk was used for dresses in well-to-do circles, cotton being considered suitable only for morning wear. According to *Cassell's Household Guide*, published in England in the 1870s, patchwork made from cotton had become an 'old-fashioned thing', suitable only for 'inferior rooms of the house', but patchwork 'made of pieces of silk and satin is

handsome, especially if arranged with taste'. Tartan fabrics are frequently found in these quilts – a taste led by Queen Victoria's love of all things Scottish. Doubtless, patchwork from silk, which made beautiful, glowing quilts and covers, was the province of women who were better off and thus had access to the fabric and time for leisure sewing.

Late in the nineteenth century, Log Cabin quilts were made all around Australia. While Log Cabin quilts were made in England, it was also a very popular style in Ireland. The Log Cabin technique is done by starting with a centre square and then successively adding strips around and around to make a larger square. Many such squares are sewn, then joined together to make the quilt. By placing dark strips on one half of each square and light strips on the other half, patterns are created when the squares are joined together. Very small and narrow strips of fabric could be used, so it was an ideal way for using scraps, and most Log Cabin quilts were made of a large variety of fabrics.

DETAIL OF SILK PIECED BABY BLOCK PATTERN *(top left), second half of the nineteenth century. Private collection.* DETAIL OF LOG CABIN *(top right), made by the Smith sisters, Hall, New South Wales (now part of the Australian Capital Territory), around 1900. Private collection.*

MIKE FISHER

MIKE FISHER

DETAIL OF CRAZY PATCHWORK (top). *Made by the Lydiard family, Victoria, 1894. Private collection.*
WOOL CRAZY QUILT (above), *Tasmania, 1930s. 160 cm x 210 cm (63 in x 83 in). Private collection.*

Usually, although not always, the Log Cabin was constructed onto a foundation fabric, with a square of scrap fabric used as a base for the sewing. This foundation square also made an extra layer in the quilt.

After 1890, crazy patchwork was a very popular style throughout Australia, and it was a style which persisted through into the 1950s. Crazy patchwork is made by taking odd and random-shaped patches of fabric and overlaying them onto a foundation fabric. Sometimes the foundation was the size of the quilt, or sometimes it was a square which was joined with other squares to make a quilt. Usually, embroidery was added around the edge of each patch, both to decorate and hold the patch in place. More decorative embroidery was often added, so that the whole became an elaborate confection of stitching. People embroidered names, initials and motifs that were important to them. Other typical motifs which are found on crazy quilts include flowers, butterflies, teapots, horseshoes and tennis racquets. Some quilts have figures in outline embroidery which are in the style of Kate Greenaway, an English illustrator of children's books, who drew people dressed in eighteenth century clothing. These figures were popular motifs for embroidery at the time. The example on this page is a piece of crazy patchwork handed down in the Lydiard family, and has the date 1894 stitched on it. It illustrates the personal nature of crazy patchwork. The name 'J.H.S. Lydiard' is clear; other names and initials relate to family names. Tandarook and Caulfield are place names from Victoria found on the quilt. The Lydiards were a prominent pastoralist family in Victoria, and were related to the explorer Charles Sturt. However, it is not known who actually made the crazy patchwork.

Later crazy quilts tend to be more simple and functional than the elaborate and decorative quilts from the 1890s. Wool or cotton fabrics were used for these later crazy quilts, with simpler embroidery added.

Embroidered quilts are seen from the turn of the century through until the end of the Second World War. The quilts are made by adding embroidery to

squares of fabric, then sewing the squares together
– although sometimes the embroidery is added to
larger pieces of fabric. In the late nineteenth
century, red embroidery on a white or cream background became fashionable, and this is the most
typical colour combination used. Signature quilts,
in which signatures are embroidered, are a type of
embroidered quilt, and these were often made to
raise money by charging a small fee for each signature,
or else made as memorials to a group of people.

Utility quilts were simply pieced out of whatever
material women had on hand – woollen scraps,
commercial fabric samples, pieces of knitwear, left-
overs from dressmaking, and parts of cut-up old
clothing. For example, one Australian quilt of the
1960s was made of squares of fabric from a
swimwear factory where the woman worked. The
shapes used were usually simple-to-sew squares,
rectangles and, occasionally, triangles. Most
frequently found of this type of patchwork
was made from woollen suiting samples. Women
obtained outdated samples from tailors and
drapers, especially in country towns where
men's suits were ordered from sample books.
The suiting sample patchwork bedcovers were
not usually called quilts, but were called rugs.
Although mainly functional, and often made
for hard-wearing situations, such as boys'
beds, it is rare to find one of these utility
bedcovers which does not show that care
was taken to arrange the fabrics into some
simple pattern, such as alternating lighter
and darker colours, or even to adding a
decorative touch through embroidery.

The Wagga rug was a particular kind
of utility quilt made in Australia. There
are two types of Wagga rugs: those
made by men and those made by
women. Wagga rugs made by men con-
sisted of three or five (depending on their size) jute
wheat bags stitched together with twine. They were
used by men camping outdoors while working on
jobs like droving or fencing. The name 'Wagga rug'
has been in use at least since the 1890s, as Henry
Lawson mentions shearers having Wagga rugs in a

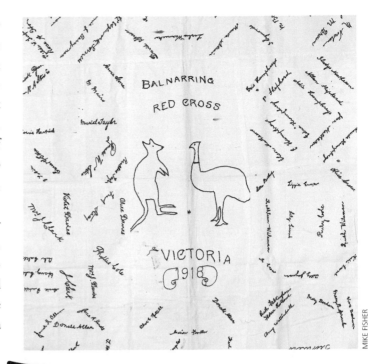

MIKE FISHER

MIKE FISHER

DETAIL OF EMBROIDERED QUILT *(top),*
Balnarring, Victoria, 1918.
SUITING SAMPLE QUILT *(above), 1903.*
180 cm x 194 cm (71 in x 77 in). Private collection.

11

MIKE FISHER

story, published in 1893. The name 'wagga' appears to derive from the town called Wagga Wagga in central New South Wales, a major centre for wheat production. The Australian love for inventing slang could easily account for the name 'wagga' being attached to the makeshift covers created out of wheat bags from the district. In contrast, Wagga rugs made by women were for domestic use. Pieces of old clothes or bedding were laid flat and roughly stitched onto a foundation of some sort, sometimes hessian or opened-out bags, but old blankets or other recycled material were also used. Worn-out woollen clothes were usually used for their warmth. This was then covered with either a cheap cotton fabric, such as cretonne, or sometimes a cover was made from simple patchwork. The recycled filling of such bedcovers is not at all obvious at first glance, but is revealed by investigating what lies beneath the outer layer. The inner layers often feel rather lumpy, and the whole is very heavy — 'lead blankets' one family called them. While poverty may have been the reason why some Wagga rugs were made, it was the general habit of thrift which made them widespread. This was a society that valued the ability to 'make something from nothing'. While the name 'wagga' is quintessentially Australian, construction of bedcovers from used clothing in this manner was not unique to Australia, as similar bedcovers were made in Britain. Also, some families made bedcovers using the same technique, but did not call them waggas.

Suffolk Puffs is a style of patchwork that was first found around the turn of the century. Circles of fabric are cut out, a running stitch hem is sewn around the outside, then the stitching is gathered up to make a small 'puff'. Hundreds of these puffs are

DOMESTIC WAGGA *(top left), Tasmania, around 1950. 134 cm x 161 cm (53 in x 63 in). Private Collection.* DETAIL OF WAGGA *(left), showing the inner woollen layers.*

sewn together to make a quilt. Early quilts of this type are usually made from all-white fabrics. There is a persistent story that the patches for these quilts came from the blue bags which were used in the final rinse of washing to whiten whites. A blue bag consisted of a lump of ultramarine blue, wrapped and tied into a square of white fabric. However, the squares of fabric used in blue bags had a very coarse weave to allow the blue to dissolve into the water, and close examination of white Suffolk Puff quilts usually shows that all kinds of white fabrics were used, mostly with close weaves. As women sewed bed linen, nightwear, baby clothes and underwear from white cotton fabrics, it seems more probable that scraps of this household sewing were mostly used for the white Suffolk Puffs. Later Suffolk Puff quilts were usually made from print fabrics, and often fabric samples were used. Samples can be recognised when the same print pattern appears in several different colourways in a quilt.

In appliqué quilts, a patch of fabric is sewn to a background, a style which gives great freedom of design and lends itself to pictorial motifs. Sometimes appliqué is combined with patchwork, so an appliqué motif can be surrounded by pieced shapes, or already-pieced shapes can be appliquéd to a larger background. The edges of the patch to be appliquéd can be turned under and sewn down, or the raw edges can be sewn with a herringbone or blanket stitch. Broderic Perse, seen in a few of the very old quilts, is a kind of this latter method of appliqué in which motifs are cut from printed fabrics, especially chintz, and sewn to the background.

Beyond these recognisable styles, there is the odd quilt which does not fit into any category, such as one quilt which combined pieced squares held together with crochet.

Quilting, the stitching which holds the layers of a quilt together, is most often absent from Australian quilts prior to the mid-1970s, and none of the great decorative quilting traditions of northern England and Wales seems to have been practised here. While there are a few quilted quilts to be found, these tend to be the exceptions. Some quilts have flat quilting, which means there is

ANDREW SIKORSKI

BICA PHOTOGRAPHICS

DETAIL OF SUFFOLK PUFFS (top), around 1900. *Private collection.*
DETAIL OF APPLIQUE (above). *Made by Mrs Brown, Bowning, New South Wales, late nineteenth century. Collection Museum of Applied Arts and Sciences, Sydney.*

ANDREW PAYNE

ANDREW PAYNE

quilting holding a top and backing together, but with no padding in between. As flat quilting is very typical of Irish quilts, Australians may have been influenced by Irish practices. Some Australian quilts have a minimum of simple quilting, such as waggas which have widely spaced machine-stitching holding the layers together. Some quilts are only partially quilted, such as having quilting which only goes through the back and padding, but not going through all three layers.

After 1970, American-style piecing and quilting began to be widely introduced. This style of piecing generally involves seaming the patches together into blocks, the American term for the usually square units of patchwork. The blocks follow well-defined traditional American patterns which had names such as 'Evening Star' or 'Bear's Paw'. The blocks are then joined together to make a quilt, sometimes with strips of fabric, called sashing, in between.

Quilting, the stitching of the three layers of a quilt, became widespread. The quilting could be simple lines or outlines of the patchwork and appliqué, or it could be elaborate motifs and decorative patterns. Machine-quilting became popular and, in the 1990s, commercial quilting machines were imported so that women could send their patchwork tops away to have them quilted with

wide rows of decorative machine-stitching.

As well as the quilts made in Australia, many quilts were brought to Australia. The majority of early settlers came from Britain and Ireland, and some brought their quilts with them. Some quilts have come as family heirlooms with people who have immigrated here more recently, again primarily coming from Britain, but there are other quilts as well. For example, a few quilts have come here with Italian migrants who settled in Australia after the Second World War, and there are quilts which have accompanied Americans living in Australia. Whether they came to Australia over a century ago or just recently, some glorious quilts have found their way to Australia and now belong here. For example, an English family who came to Australia in the 1950s brought a quilt made by a great-grandmother and great-great grandmother, Mary and Martha Randall (who became Martha Winn after her marriage). Against a background of appliquéd patches of printed chintz, Mary and

DETAIL PIECED BLOCK *(top left), from 'Where Eagles Dare'. Made by Kerry Gavin, see page 91.*
DETAIL OF QUILTING *(top right), by Kerry Gavin, as above.*
QUILT MADE BY MARY AND MARTHA RANDALL *(right), England, 1891. 230 cm x 270 cm (91 in x 106 in). Private collection.*

Martha stitched the Crystal Palace and the Eiffel Tower, two of the great structures of the nineteenth century. They also appliquéd other motifs, such as a church, dogs, horses, birds, a cat, a hot-air balloon, and many crosses. The edge of the quilt is scalloped and finished with a narrow binding in Turkey-red fabric. The quilt has the date 1891 appliquéd on it, just two years after the opening of the Eiffel tower in Paris. The quilt is not padded or backed.

Other quilts in Australia exist without any known history attached to them: orphans with no clues as to who made them or where. Some of these are wonderful quilts, such as a quilt belonging to the National Trust in South Australia which was for many years displayed on a bed at Ayers House, Adelaide. A quilt which by style and fabrics belongs to the middle of the nineteenth century, it combines appliqué and piecing, the latter in the form of rosettes of hexagons. The quilt has become well-known for its beautiful border of 'dancing dollies', stylised figures each made from a large triangle for the dress, a circle for the head, and curved patches for the arms. There is some magnificent chintz in the centre appliqué and in the border fabrics outlining the major areas of the quilt.

While Australia may not have the abundance of quilts found in America, or the wealth of old quilts found in Britain and Ireland, the heritage is not insignificant. From early days to the present, Australian women have made quilts. For some it was a case of thrift, creating something from scraps that may otherwise have been thrown away. For some it was a way of helping others. But for most it was more than thrift or charity, with hours spent creating quilts which were intended to be both beautiful and useful. Through their quilts, women expressed their lives.

All history is a selection, and this book is no exception. Many more quilts exist around Australia than could be shown here. The quilts chosen have been selected to represent the major styles, to show quilts which are outstanding in terms of their design, and to illustrate important aspects of Australian society.

MICHAEL KLUVANEK

QUILT FROM AYERS HOUSE *(left), mid-nineteenth century. 243 cm x 274 cm (97 in x 108 in). National Trust of Australia (South Australia).*

THE
ABORIGINAL
HERITAGE

ABORIGINAL WOMAN WITH SKIN RUG. *Collection National Library of Australia, Canberra.*

For uncounted thousands of years, Aboriginal people lived in the large, harsh, and mostly dry continent of Australia. They knew and loved the land, with its diversity of climates and wildlife, and tribal cultures were adapted to the land and its oftentimes scarce bounty. Aboriginal people were adept at reading the minute details of their environment with a knowledge and sensitivity that totally escaped the later-arriving Europeans.

While much of Australia has either a tropical or

Mediterranean climate, the south-east of Australia and the highlands have a cool temperate climate with cold winters. The making of warm body coverings was thus a necessity, and this need was filled by making a form of patchwork rug of animal skins

Writing in 1881, James Dawson described the wearing and manufacture of such rugs in western Victoria. He noted that in cold weather the men wore a large kangaroo skin as a mantle, and sometimes 'a small rug made of a dozen skins of the opossum or young kangaroo'. The women used 'the opossum rug at all times, by day as a covering for the back and shoulders, and in cold nights as a blanket'. A kangaroo skin was substituted in wet weather. For bedding in cold weather a wallaby or opossum rug was used, in addition to dry grass.

James Dawson described the making of these rugs:

Fur rugs were very scarce and valuable before the white man destroyed the wild dogs, the natural enemies of the opossum and kangaroo, as it took a year to collect opossum skins sufficient to make one. The ring-tailed opossums were more plentiful than the common kind, but the skins were less esteemed. Rugs were also made of the skins of the wallaby and of the brush kangaroo, which are likewise inferior to the common opossum. A good rug is made from fifty to seventy skins, which are stripped off the opossum, pegged out square or oblong on a sheet of bark, and dried before the fire, then trimmed with a reed knife, and sewn together with the tail sinews of the kangaroo, which are always pulled out of the tail, and carefully dried and saved for thread. Previous to sewing the skins together, diagonal lines, about half-an-inch apart, are scratched across the flesh side of each with sharpened mussel shells. This is done to make them soft and pliable.

Nineteenth century drawings and pictures of Aboriginal people show them wearing these skin rugs, sometimes with the fur side out and sometimes with the scratched skin side out. Designs were also added to the scratchings in some rugs.

Skin rugs are seen in a photograph of an Aboriginal woman which was taken about 1870. It is most probably a posed photograph, and it is believed to be of Charlotte Wheler of the Kiewa River tribe, Victoria. One surviving Aboriginal skin rug is in the collection of the Museum of Victoria. The skins of this rug are closely stitched together and there are a variety of patterns scratched and painted on the skin side.

European settlers were quick to recognise the value of the skin rugs. In 1842, a 'Lady' wrote of them: 'Every settler, when riding through the bush, carries a kangaroo rug or a blanket fastened before him on his horse so that, wherever he goes, he is provided with his bed.'

Mrs Clacy wrote about opossum rugs after her visit to the Victorian goldfields in 1852. Opossum rugs had been purchased as part of her party's equipment for travelling in Australia and, when she was returning to England by ship, the rugs were used in the cold weather around Cape Horn:

We were glad to avail ourselves of our opossum rugs to keep ourselves warm. One of these rugs is quite sufficient covering of a night in the coldest weather, and imparts as much heat as a dozen blankets. They are made from the skins of the opossums, sewn together by the natives with sinews of the same animal.

She wrote that scarcity of these rugs due to high demand during the gold rush had increased the price from two sovereigns to ten pounds.

Following the model of the Aboriginal rugs, Australians made skin rugs in the nineteenth and twentieth century by tanning hides of both native animals and introduced ones, such as foxes. Many such rugs were made around country Australia, and usually the skins were backed with woollen baize.

While they were not made of woven fabric, these rugs are a form of sewn patchwork, and they demonstrate a heritage which existed long before the Europeans came. It was a heritage that the Europeans were quick to adopt and adapt to their own purposes.

1788 TO 1850

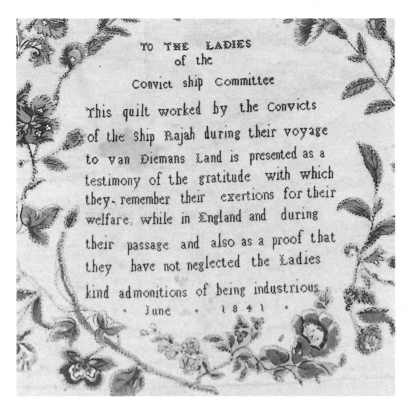

TO THE LADIES
of the
Convict ship Committee
This quilt worked by the Convicts
of the ship Rajah during their voyage
to van Diemans Land is presented as a
testimony of the gratitude with which
they. remember their exertions for their
welfare, while in England and during
their passage and also as a proof that
they have not neglected the Ladies
kind admonitions of being industrious
· June · 1841 ·

DETAIL OF QUILT MADE BY CONVICT WOMEN.
Collection National Gallery of Australia, Canberra. See page 21.

Over the centuries, the Terra Australis Incognita, the Great South Land with all its Aboriginal inhabitants, was only occasionally visited by European explorers. In 1770, the British expedition led by Captain Cook visited the east coast and claimed it for Britain. Based on the favourable recommendation from Cook's expedition and the overt need to find a new place to send prisoners from the overcrowded gaols and prison hulks in England, the British government decided to establish a penal colony in New South Wales. Governor Phillip and the First Fleet arrived at Botany Bay in January 1788, and quickly moved the settlement site to Sydney Cove and the better harbour of Port Jackson. A little more than a thousand people, including about seven hundred convicts, assembled on 26 January for the raising of the Union Flag of Britain (Union Jack as it is today).

From insecure beginnings bedevilled by uncertain supplies, the difficulties of initially establishing agriculture, and corruption among the military officers, the little colony managed to survive and, by the 1820s, began to thrive. Free settlers began arriving and exploration of the vast hinterland was undertaken, revealing land that was especially suitable for grazing. In 1803, settlement was begun in Van Diemen's Land, the large island to the south which later became known as Tasmania. From the late 1820s, some tentative settlements were begun in other places around the Australian coastline, and the successful ones led to the eventual creation of the colonies of Victoria, South Australia and Western Australia.

Throughout this period, Australia was a penal colony and the original reason for settlement remained important. Between 1788 and 1852, some one hundred and sixty thousand convicts were transported to eastern Australia. The larger portion of these were sent to New South Wales, but a substantial number were sent to Van Diemen's Land. Many more men than women were transported, but altogether almost twenty-four thousand women were sent. Conditions for the convicts ranged from brutal to tolerable, the treatment depending on the concern or neglect of the officers in charge. Gradually conditions were improved as regulations were introduced to ensure better care.

In England, Elizabeth Fry became involved in prison reform. Elizabeth was a wealthy and devout member of the Society of Friends, more usually known as Quakers. She first visited Newgate prison in 1813, and was appalled at the condition of the women and children. The demands of her own large and growing family claimed Elizabeth until 1816, but then she began suggesting prison reforms to the authorities. She realised that what the women most needed was some kind of occupation. She wrote that 'I soon found that nothing could be done, or was worth attempting for the reformation of the women, without constant employment'. Elizabeth organised a committee of twelve women, almost all Quakers, called 'The Association for the Improvement of the Female Prisoners in Newgate'. They determined to visit the prison daily, to pay a salary for a matron, to provide money for work and to clothe the women. They also determined to teach them religious principles; to 'introduce them to a knowledge of Holy Scriptures and to form in them, as much as possible, habits of order, sobriety and industry which may render them docile and peaceable while in prison, and respectable when they leave it'. Useful needlework was the way in which the prisoners could be employed, and could earn them some money towards the day when they would be released. The 'habit of industry' was the important virtue that the committee most wished the women to learn.

The authorities, although sceptical, agreed to try Mrs Fry's reformist ideas. Quaker merchants were persuaded to supply materials, and the first project undertaken was a patchwork quilt, although the major work soon became sewing clothing and knitting stockings.

Mrs Fry organised the prisoners into classes of twelve, each with a monitor, and cleanliness and order were insisted on. The change in the prisoners was immediately apparent, and it became fashionable for society people to visit Newgate to hear Elizabeth Fry read to the prisoners. An 1820 account describes the tidy and well-ordered prisoners listening to the Bible, and the matron showing the articles that the women had made: 'caps, dressing gowns, baby-linen, bags, rugs, patch-work, counterpanes of elegant designs, etc. also stockings, baskets, etc.'

Elizabeth Fry also became aware of the crowded and intolerable conditions that the prisoners faced when they left Newgate for transportation to Botany Bay. Again she instituted reforms, beginning in 1818 with the ship *Maria*. Instead of being shackled in irons and put into open carts, the women were conveyed to the ship in closed hackney coaches. On board ship, the women were divided into groups of twelve, with a monitor, in the same way that they had been organised in Newgate. To provide occupation for the long voyage, sewing utensils and patchwork materials were supplied. The quilt made during the journey could be sold on arrival in the colony, or even en route, providing the women with a little money to help them become established in the new land. Women of the *Wellington* found they could sell their quilts for a guinea each in Rio de Janeiro, a port where the ship called on the way to Australia.

The British Society of Ladies, as the committee became known, supplied each convict woman with a Bible and a variety of useful things, including:

a small hessian bag that contained: one piece of tape; one oz. of pins; one hundred needles; four balls of white sewing cotton; one ditto black; one ditto blue; one ditto red; two balls of black worsted, half an oz. each; twenty-four hanks of colored thread, one of cloth, with 8 darning needles and one small bodkin fastened on it; two stay laces; one thimble; one pair of scissors; one pair of spectacles, when required; two lbs. of patch-work pieces.

Writing in 1827, Elizabeth Fry said, 'Formerly, patchwork occupied much of the time of the women confined in Newgate, as it still does that of the female convicts on the voyage to New South Wales. It is an unexceptionable mode of employing female prisoners, if no other work can be procured, and is useful as a means of teaching them the art of sewing.'

She continued to visit and help organise the women on ships leaving for Botany Bay until 1841. She died not long after, in 1843.

The majority of quilts made by the convict women were either used for themselves, or sold to other people for use, and thus were worn out. The women would not have had sentimental reasons to keep them, and most probably would have actively not wanted reminders of their former convict past. However, one convict-made quilt has survived, and the new condition of some of its fabrics suggests that it has probably never been used. The quilt was found in Scotland, and possibly it was sent from Australia to England soon after its making, although nothing is known about the history of the quilt from its arrival in Australia until its discovery in the 1980s.

The quilt is made in the medallion style, with successive pieced and appliquéd borders which surround a centre of Broderie Perse appliqué. The piecing shows the work of many hands, as the quality and style of stitching vary enormously.

QUILT MADE BY CONVICT WOMEN. *325 cm x 337 cm (128 in x 133 in). Collection National Gallery of Australia, Canberra.*

A very large quilt, its borders have been added to borders, without regard for measurement, so the final borders are over-full and do not sit flat. One side of the quilt has an embroidered inscription which reads:

To the ladies of the convict ship committee
This quilt worked by the Convicts of the ship Rajah during their voyage to Van Diemans Land is presented as a testimony of the gratitude with which they remember their exertions for their welfare while in England and during their passage and also as a proof that they have not neglected the Ladies kind admonition of being industrious.
June 1841

21

The quilt was sewn by women on board the *Rajah*, which left England on 5 April 1841, and arrived in Van Diemen's Land on 19 July. The *Rajah* carried one hundred and seventy-nine prisoners, ten children, and several passengers, which included the Rev. R. Davis and Miss Kezia Hayter. According to a report sent back to the Society of Ladies:

The prisoners in the Rajah were peculiarly favoured. A clergyman who was returning to his duties in the colony, went out in that ship as a passenger. Beside the advantage which the prisoners derived from the instruction given by the clergyman, they were also under the superintendence of a female of superior attainments, who had previously been an officer at the General Penitentiary, and who obtained a free passage in the Rajah with the understanding that she should devote her time during the voyage to the improvement of the convicts.

Putting all this information together, it may well have been Miss Kezia Hayter who instigated the making of the quilt, and sewed the obsequious inscription. The beautiful needlework and language used suggest the hand of 'a female of superior attainments', and, moreover, Miss Hayter may have been anxious to prove to the ladies' committee how well she earned her free passage. What better way than sending back a quilt of the pieces of fabric they had provided, with a message that rewards the ladies' endeavours?

On 23 July, Lady Jane Franklin, the wife of the governor of Van Diemen's Land, mentioned the quilt in her diary notes, 'quilt displayed with marking ins[criptio]n for Ladies of Committee — Sir J. s[ai]d very well done'. Lady Jane Franklin was anxious to become involved in the reforms for the convict women, influenced by Mrs Fry's prescriptions. She attempted to set up her own committee of ladies in Hobart and caused a local controversy for herself and for Miss Hayter. On the arrival of the *Rajah*, Lady Jane had also noted Miss Hayter's engagement to Captain Ferguson, the master of the *Rajah*. The couple were married in Hobart, 1 July 1843.

Altogether, one hundred and six ships and twelve thousand convicts passed through Mrs Fry's hands, so presumably many, many quilts must have been made. One grateful convict woman, transported on the *Brothers* in 1823, sent a calabash as a present intended for Mrs Fry. It arrived in 1843, after Elizabeth Fry's death earlier that year. With the gift was a message that the woman had been married for twenty years, and had 'plenty of pigs and fowls, buys her tea by the chest; and the patchwork quilt which now covers her bed, was made of the pieces given her by the ladies when she embarked.'

The convicts were accompanied by civil and military officers and by soldiers. The New South Wales Corps was formed to provide order in the colony, and members of the corps first arrived with the Second Fleet in 1790. Amongst the officers was Lieutenant John Macarthur, who brought with him his wife, Elizabeth, and their son, Edward. On the six-month journey to New South Wales, a baby daughter was born prematurely and died.

John Macarthur was a talented but difficult man, ambitious to make his fortune in the new land, but oblivious to all points of view other than his own. Given good land at Parramatta, he soon established

ELIZABETH MACARTHUR (above). *Courtesy of Camden Park Preservation Committee.*
QUILT ATTRIBUTED TO ELIZABETH MACARTHUR *(top right), 272 cm x 285 cm (107 in x 112 in). Collection National Trust, New South Wales.*

a thriving farm which he named Elizabeth Farm after his wife. His farming activities and entrepreneurial flair made Macarthur perceive the possibilities for wool production in the colony. A turbulent man in public life, he fell out with every successive governor, and in 1801 was sent back to England for a court martial after a duel with the Lieutenant Governor, Colonel Paterson. Macarthur was involved in the so-called 'Rum Rebellion', in which officers of the New South Wales Corps took over the government after their corrupt monopolies and trade in rum were challenged by Governor Bligh. In 1808, Macarthur was again sent to England and was exiled there until 1817, during which time he resigned from the army. Macarthur used the times he was in England to promote the wool industry in the colony, and each time was eventually able to return to Australia. The English government rewarded his pastoral activities with more land and access to the purchase of some rare Spanish Merino sheep from the royal flock. The land granted to Macarthur was taken at Cowpastures,

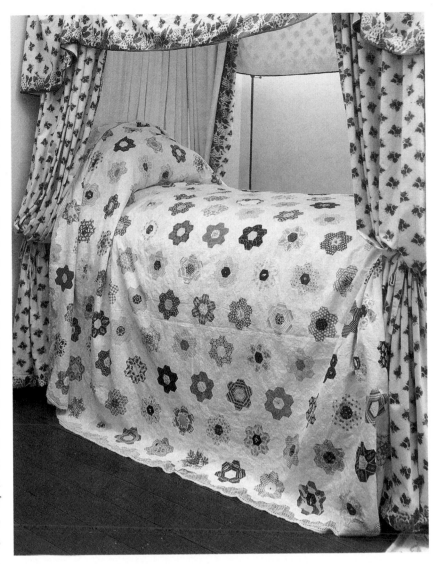

later called Camden after the then Secretary of State. By the 1820s, high prices were paid for the fine Macarthur wool shipped to England, and in 1822, Macarthur was awarded medals for his contribution to the wool industry. His activities had done a great deal to establish a lucrative future for wool growing in Australia.

Throughout all this, John's wife, Elizabeth, remained in Australia and managed the family's growing agricultural interests during the many years he was away. Although she found looking after the estates 'troublesome … in the extreme', John made reference to Elizabeth's 'prudent and able management'. Elizabeth and John had nine children, three of whom died in infancy or early childhood. The sons and eldest daughter were sent back to England for their education. Known as a

calm and practical person, Elizabeth was a contrast to her tempestuous husband. In the last years of his life John Macarthur's mental and physical health declined, and fears for Elizabeth's safety from his violent and deranged temper meant that they had to live apart. John Macarthur died in 1834. Supported by her family, Elizabeth remained at Elizabeth Farm, the home she loved, and died in February 1850.

A hexagon patchwork quilt has been attributed to Elizabeth Macarthur. The quilt is finely stitched from cotton fabrics, and consists of rosettes of hexagons from print materials set into a background of plain cream hexagons. The hexagons have been carefully cut and sewn so that stripes go in determined directions and motifs are centred within the patches. The quilt is unlined, and may never have been finished. Elizabeth was an able woman with the needle and participated in sewing for her family. Her son Edward, who spent much of his life in England, ordered muslins to be sent out for the girls' dresses, and Elizabeth insisted on good-quality fabric. Elizabeth would have had the time and leisure to sew such a quilt, especially in the later years of her life when the quilt was most probably made. Elizabeth's daughter Mary, married James Bowman, and the quilt has been handed down through generations of descendants in the Bowman family.

As exploration proceeded and agricultural lands were opened up, the Aboriginal people were further and further dispossessed of the land. When they reacted with anger and attacked either settlers or their herds, retribution was swift and awful. They also were decimated by European diseases such as measles and were debilitated by alcohol. A few benevolent, but nevertheless paternalistic, people pondered the fate of the Aboriginal people, and one such person was Colonel Irwin who was the first military commandant of Western Australia. Arriving on the *Sulphur* in 1829, he returned to England in 1833 where he married Elizabeth Courthope. The Irwins returned to Western Australia in 1837 and finally left in 1854. During this time Elizabeth bore ten children. Colonel Irwin was an important man in the new colony and was Acting Governor briefly from 1832 to 1833, and again from 1847 to 1848. He was a stern, religious man and actively promoted the Church of England and temperance. Concerned about the Aboriginal people, in his book *The State and Position of Western Australia, commonly Called the Swan-River Settlement*, he wrote:

The author cannot let this opportunity pass without calling the attention of the public to the claims which the natives of New Holland have upon it. It must be confessed that to those tribes, hitherto, British example and connexion have, for the most part, been found very reverse of beneficial. It is impossible for a moment to maintain or vindicate the abstract right of civilised nations to establish themselves in the territories of savage tribes, without, at least, acknowledging that such intrusions involve the settlers, and

the nation to which they belong, in deep and lasting responsibilities; in other words, that the latter are bound, by the strongest ties of moral obligation to assist the natives in accommodating themselves to the great changes they would have to undergo; for it is incumbent upon us ever to bear in mind that, by our entry, and establishment in the country, the natives are gradually deprived of their hunting and fishing grounds, and are consequently forced, unprepared, into new modes of life, and new conditions of society.

A little medallion-style quilt would seem to be associated with his concerns. Colonel Irwin had a niece, Elizabeth Irwin, who is believed to have supervised the sewing of the quilt sometime around 1840. The patchwork quilt was given to the National Library, along with the following story, handwritten by Mary Willis, the donor:

This patchwork quilt became mine in 1921[.] I kept it as I found it, hoping some day it may find its way back to Australia where many years ago it was sewn together by Aborigine children, they were taught to sew by a young English Lady, Miss Elizabeth Irwin, who also held a Sunday Sch[ool] and taught them to read etc. Miss E. Irwin was a niece of Colonel Irwin (who was then Commandant of the troops in West Australia)[,] she joined Col I[.] and was companion to Mrs Irwin and I believe lived at Perth. W.A. I met Miss E. Irwin once; she was then a frail old Lady.

Mary Willis had looked after a Miss Jane Nixon in her old age. Jane and her sister Eliza had been nursemaids to the Irwin family during the time they lived at the Swan River colony, then the sisters returned to England with the family in the 1850s. The little quilt was apparently amongst Jane's possessions when she died in England in 1921. Mary Willis had enjoyed Jane's stories of colonial life, including a story about a pet wallaby who would join the children for tea in the nursery.

Influenced by her uncle's beliefs, Elizabeth Irwin may have endeavoured to teach the Aboriginal children, and sewing would have been seen as one of the skills of 'civilisation'. The quilt is a typical medallion quilt, with frames of simple shapes surrounding a four-pointed star in the centre. The

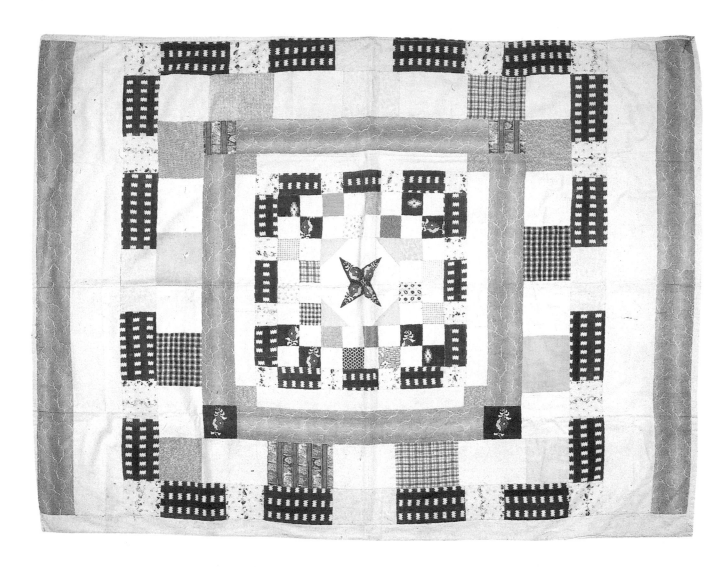

QUILT MADE BY ABORIGINAL CHILDREN.
105 cm x 140 cm (41 in x 55 in). Collection National Library of Australia, Canberra.

sewing has been done by oversewing and is uneven in quality. A lining of white cotton has been crudely stitched on by machine and is most probably a later addition.

By 1850, Australia had become a series of well-established colonies, even though there had been a severe recession during the 1840s. Great pasture lands had been opened up for sheep grazing and free immigrants had come to outnumber the convicts. It was still very much a frontier society, however, with more men than women. In 1850, there were one hundred and forty-three men for every one hundred women, and the authorities tried to entice women in Britain to emigrate to redress the balance.

Probably few quilts were made in Australia during these early years. Patchwork was the province of the class called 'ladies', such as Elizabeth Macarthur, and there were very few of these. Most of the patchwork made was what 'ladies' benevolently imposed on those they considered to be lower classes, such as the convicts or Aboriginal children. The sewing of such patchwork aimed to teach them skills and habits of industry, and may well not have been what these people would have chosen to do themselves.

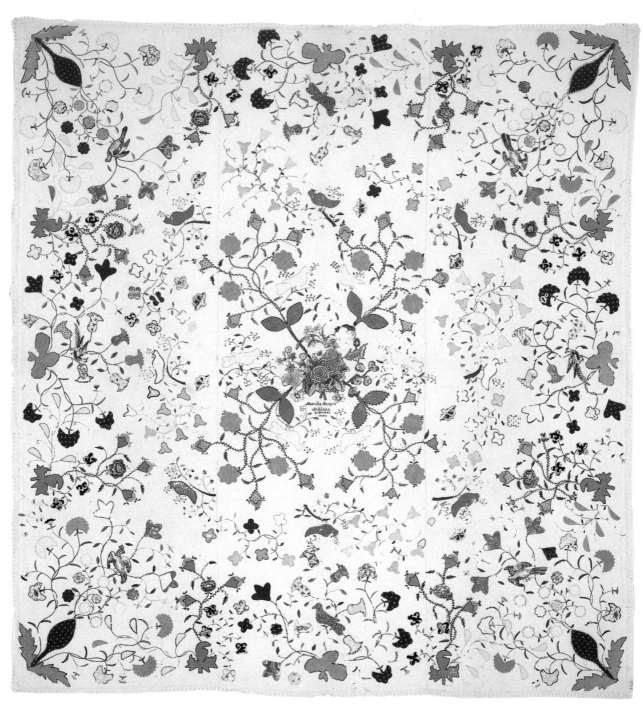

MIKE FISHER

QUILT MADE BY MARTHA BERGIN.
244 cm x 256 cm (96 in x 101 in). Private collection.

1851 TO 1889

DETAIL OF QUILT.

The discovery of gold changed everything for Australia. Discoveries were first made near Bathurst in New South Wales in 1851 and then at Clunes and Ballarat in Victoria. Australia immediately became appealing as a destination for those seeking to better their lives quickly. The population boomed and a great wealth of gold was discovered. In just one decade, from 1851 to 1861, the Australian population rose from under half a million to over a million, and one hundred million pounds worth of gold was found in Victoria.

People flooded to the goldfields, some to find gold, many to dig in vain, and others to make gold by setting up in businesses which catered for the diggers' needs. While there were many more men than women on the goldfields, there were some women.

One young couple, Andrew Tipping and his wife, Martha, had a quilt with them in their travels around the goldfields. Andrew Tipping married Martha Bergin on 26 May 1846, in Athlone. He was just twenty-two and she was twenty-four. Before her marriage she had made a large appliqué quilt, in the centre of which she embroidered her name, the town where she lived, and the date, 1843. The embroidery on the inscription is done in exquisite cross stitch. Just one layer of cream cloth, with the appliqué shapes buttonhole-stitched on top, the quilt is a glorious riot of appliquéd birds, flowers and leaves, with tendrils and stems embroidered in wool. Some of the motifs have been cut out of chintz fabric, Broderie-Perse fashion, but others are silhouettes cut from ordinary prints. The existence in Ireland of a quilt with similar motifs suggests there may have been some common or shared patterns. Martha's father was a draper in Rathdowney, so she would have had ready access to scraps of fabric for her quilt.

The story of Martha and her family becomes unclear for a few years after her marriage. A son, Simon, was born, and it is known that she visited the United States because she and her son were listed as arriving in New York in 1848, although no mention is made of Andrew. Ireland had endured a devastating famine from 1845 to 1847, when the potato, the staple food of the ordinary people of Ireland, was struck with disease. Around a million people died of starvation and another one and a half million left Ireland, so it is not surprising that Martha may have been one of many Irish people leaving home to look for a better life elsewhere. Another son, William, was born around this time.

In 1851, Martha and Andrew Tipping took assisted passages to Australia, part of an emigration scheme funded by a vote from the House of Commons. As the children are not listed, it is assumed that they must have both died. Martha and Andrew sailed on the ship *Beulah* from Plymouth, and arrived in Hobart Town, Van Diemen's Land, on 29 August. While the emigration schemes favoured single women in order to help redress the balance of the sexes in Australia, some married couples were also brought out to act as chaperones. On the ship, Andrew was engaged as a constable and was paid £2. The *Register of Arrivals* records that Andrew and Martha 'secured employment with Mr William Murray of Liverpool Street for £40 per annum', the highest amount of pay offered to any of the couples.

Martha and Andrew did not stay in Van Diemen's Land very long. By 1852, their son James was born in Melbourne and was baptised in St Francis' Church. In 1855, their fourth son, John Joseph, was born and then died in Melbourne. After this, their movements can be followed around the goldfields by the births and deaths of further children. A son, Andrew, was born at Fiery Creek in 1856. A daughter, Martha, was born at Back Creek in 1859. Mary Anne was born and died at Landsborough in 1862. In 1863, the family was in Dunolly where two children, Martha and Andrew, both died. Andrew senior was described on the children's death certificates as a 'digger', so evidently he had been trying his luck with the various rushes to places where gold was discovered in Victoria. Later in life, James, the only survivor of Martha's seven children, mentions in his diary that he had once seen snow when the family was living on a goldfield.

Eventually, Andrew took out a freehold crown grant of some nineteen acres (seven and a half hectares) outside Bealiba, another town where gold had been found. Bealiba was a town near Moligal where the Welcome Stranger, the world's largest nugget which weighed more than two thousand three hundred ounces (about sixty-five kilograms), was found. Andrew worked on the small selection with his

son James, and also did contracting work on roads and bridges. The property was called 'Auburn Vale' after a beautiful area near Andrew's home in Ireland. Andrew died in 1882, aged fifty-eight. He had had a hard life and wrote in his son's diary of 'My sad life and miserable' after he had been robbed of clothes, bedding and boots in 1881. Martha died on 7 November 1883. She was remembered in the family as a lovely, gentle woman who was strongly attached to her only surviving son. When James's wife Mary was ill in 1881, Martha travelled from Bealiba to be with her, going by a sulky to St Arnaud, train to Melbourne, steamer to Sydney, another steamer to Merimbula, coach to Bombala, and finally by trap to Bendoc. The return journey proved even more arduous, as she was thrown out of the trap outside of Bombala, chipping a collar bone. She struggled on to Cooma, then to Goulburn, where she became very chilled in the August cold, and finally travelled by rail to Melbourne.

Andrew and Martha were buried in a double grave in the Catholic section of the Bealiba Cemetery. Throughout all this moving around, Martha's baggage contained her precious quilt, her linen, the lace cap in which she was married, and a family Bible, all of which remain within the family today.

The gold rush created jobs and money for many people who did not themselves dig for gold. Businesses, such as hotels, were developed on the roads leading to the goldfields. The Junction Hotel,

MIKE FISHER

QUILT MADE BY ELIZABETH KEEN (above). 233 cm x 266 cm (92 in x 105 in). Collection Queensliffe Historical Society, Victoria.
JUNCTION HOTEL, FYANSFORD (far left). Courtesy of Geelong Historical Society.

Fyansford, was such a business, as it was located some 4 miles (approximately 6.4 kilometres) from the port of Geelong, on Port Phillip Bay, Victoria. The hotel was situated 1 mile (1.6 kilometres) from the river crossing at Fynansford, at the junction between the road to Ballarat and the road west to the rich farming lands of the Western District in Victoria. In recent years, Alexander McFarlane, who was born at Fyansford, recalled seeing bullock wagons laden with goods passing along the road on their way to the goldfields.

Mrs Elizabeth Wensor, a widow, was the proprietor of the hotel, and in 1872 she married Charles

BRIAN BOLTON

are appliquéd in place with herringbone stitch. In the centre of the quilt, worked in wool and canvas stitch, Elizabeth Keen embroidered 'Mrs E. Keen – 1879 – Geelong – Junction Hotel – Fyansford', so that no-one would ever forget who made the quilt, and when and where. The quilt is backed with a red print which does not extend to the appliquéd border. The edge of the quilt is finished with green bias binding.

In 1882, Elizabeth's daughter, Christiana Wensor, married William Moore, a livery stable keeper, and in 1883, her daughter Elizabeth married William Eaton, also a livery stable keeper, so it certainly was a family very involved with horses. Elizabeth herself must have loved horses, to portray them so beautifully on her quilt. Perhaps the quilt, with its hearts in the corners, was made as a wedding present for one of the daughters.

The second half of the nineteenth century was the age of grand exhibitions following on from the Great Exhibition held at the Crystal Palace in London in 1851. Colonial towns, both large and small, followed the example. The Geelong Industrial and Juvenile Exhibition was held from 1879 to 1880. In the official list of awards, 'Patchwork quilts' was a category, and a silver medal and five certificates were awarded. Obviously, Mrs Keen was not the only woman stitching patchwork in Geelong at this time. However, she is not listed as obtaining an award for patchwork, but she was mentioned for an award for her crochet.

During this time, the flocks of sheep and herds of cattle increased on the vast grazing lands of Australia, and many of the squatters, the owners of these herds, grew wealthy. The term 'squatter' in Australia refers to the men who in the early days of settlement had 'squatted' on the land, and thus had claimed it for their own use. The name 'squatter' stuck and came to refer to lease- or land-holders who had large properties which came to be called 'stations'. The low rainfall has always meant that the carrying capacity of most farms in Australia was low, and therefore sheep and cattle stations were often very large in size. In New South Wales, the number of sheep grew from some five million in 1860 to a peak

Keen, a widower. Elizabeth is listed as a dressmaker on the marriage certificate, She made a magnificent pieced quilt. It contains some eleven thousand tiny pieces, with each patch sewn over paper, in the English style. The pattern she chose was an intricate one. Hundreds of small squares are sewn to make larger squares in the centre of the quilt, then these are surrounded by blocks sewn into a star pattern. All of the blocks have sashing strips of pieced squares and triangles, with appliquéd diamonds added. All kinds of fabrics were used, including silks and cottons. Not content with her masterful piecing, Elizabeth Keen added the delightful touch of little appliquéd cats in the centre of each of the star blocks and in each of the hexagons which make an inner border around the quilt. In the corners of this border there are appliquéd hearts. Around the outer border of the quilt there are beautifully appliquéd horses, each with its own embroidered harness complete with tassels and silk buttons. Both the horses and the cats of over fifty million in 1890, and it was said that Australia rode to wealth 'on the sheep's back'.

A magnificent silk quilt was made by Amy Susanna Staniforth, widow of William Staniforth who had been an eminent surgeon in Sheffield, England. The Staniforths had twelve children, and the youngest, Georgina, was born in 1833. Georgina married Henry Ricketson, who owned Aratong station near Deniliquin and Barratta station in Queensland. Henry Ricketson was to become one of the biggest landowners in New South Wales, and in the 1860s, he built a large brick homestead on Barratta. Coming to Australia in 1853, Amy spent her last years with her daughter Georgina, and died at Barratta in 1868, aged seventy-seven. Amy's body was shipped from Queensland back to Deniliquin where she was buried. A stone was also erected in her memory on Aratong station. Amy Staniforth was a woman of many accomplishments. She also wrote a book called *Australia and other Poems*, which was published privately. The sewing of silk patches being an appropriate pastime for a woman of her age and position in life, Amy probably worked on the quilt during her last years which she spent with her daughter. Amy sewed a star pattern in the centre of the quilt, then surrounded this with hexagons and diamonds sewn together to make the Baby Block pattern. An all-over pattern of Baby Blocks completes the quilt, with stars in the corners and in the centre of two sides. The quilt is lined with cream silk.

At this time Australia was still not a unified country, but was rather a series of British colonies, with major power still residing with the government in England. Most people living in Australia were British subjects, and when Queen Victoria celebrated her 50th Jubilee in 1887, there were great celebrations by her loyal Australian colonists. The *Australasian* newspaper of Melbourne reported that 'The Queen's Jubilee will be widely and enthusiastically celebrated throughout Victoria. The important towns will be illuminated and bonfires will blaze on the tops of the hills.

Addresses are now being extensively signed'. The addresses to which they referred were to be sent 'home', meaning back to England. Banners were hung in the streets of the capital cities, and statues to Queen Victoria were erected. Not quite all the people shared this enthusiasm, however: author Henry Lawson lamented that children were more likely to be able to recite the names of English sovereigns than to locate Port Phillip.

The celebration of the Jubilee is reflected in some of Australia's quilts. Mary Bruton made her quilt over many years, but finished it in the Jubilee year. Born Mary Ann Holley in 1851, in Tasmania, she married a farmer, William Bruton, at Bendigo in 1868. Altogether, Mary Ann and William Bruton had eight children. In 1885, the family moved to Swan Hill where William worked on a contract for carrying goods. While in Bendigo,

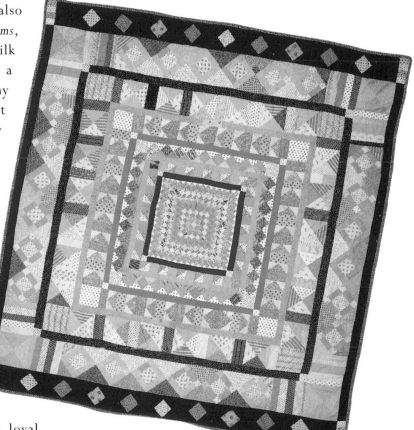

QUILT MADE BY MARY BRUTON (above).
222 cm x 238 cm (87 in x 94 in). Collection National Gallery of Australia, Canberra.
SILK QUILT MADE BY AMY STANIFORTH (far left).
116 cm x 159 cm (46 in x 63 in). Private collection.

DETAIL OF COMMEMORATIVE PRINT *(above).*
APPLIQUED AND EMBROIDERED QUILT *(right).*
224 cm x 228 cm (88 in x 90 in). Collection Tasmanian
Museum and Art Gallery.

Mary Ann worked as dressmaker and used bits of leftover cotton fabrics to make the centre of the quilt. The quilt was begun in 1873, the year that her second son was born, and the family recount that she sewed the patches together while rocking the cradle with her foot. To construct the quilt, Mary Ann Bruton put squares, rectangles and triangles together to make successive borders which she sewed, in the medallion-style, around the patchwork centre. The quilt was finished by treadle sewing machine in 1887 with fabrics specially purchased to complete it. To back the quilt, Mary Ann Bruton used a print commemorating Queen Victoria's Jubilee. The print is a repeating pattern of a small portrait of Queen Victoria surrounded by roses representing England, thistles representing Scotland, and shamrocks representing Ireland. Typical of most Australian quilts, the quilt has no batting or quilting, and the layers are held together only by the binding. The quilt was exhibited in the Kerang District Agricultural Fair in 1888 and won two first prizes. The quilt continued to win first prize for the next nine years, from 1889 to

1897, until exhibition rules were changed.

The Australian connection to the Empire is also shown in a large appliquéd and embroidered quilt, made in Tasmania around the time of the Queen's Jubilee. It is not known who made the quilt, or precisely why. It is believed that the quilt may have been won in a raffle by a member of the Radcliff family, a prominent Tasmanian family who owned the quilt for many years. In pride of place at the centre of the quilt are the Prince of Wales feathers. These are surrounded by embroidered motifs of a hand of cards, a fan, a duck and a bird. Squares of huckaback embroidery encircle this centre, the motifs including Kate Greenaway-style children, a dog, a butterfly and a house. The next round has an intriguing variety of appliquéd and embroidered motifs, including fans, flags, peacock feathers, and even a very Australian snake. There are two embroidered cartoon figures of British soldiers, one titled a 'Heavy Dragoon' who is so heavy his horse has sunk to the ground beneath him, and the other titled a 'Light Dragoon', who is so light that his horse has galloped away from underneath him. There is an appliqué of a letter showing the 'Ho' of a Hobart postmark and an address to a 'Miss Blyth, Formby'. Formby has since become part of Devonport. Both the reference to Hobart and Formby indicate the Tasmanian associations of the

quilt. A small circle with the three-legged symbol of the Isle of Man shows the date 1887 and the words 'Jubilee of Queen Victoria'. 'Tina worked this' is embroidered in one place. The quilt is finished with a magnificent border of appliquéd and embroidered fans and, between them, more butterflies, embroidered flags representing British dominions and famous British battles, and other motifs such as teacups and trays. Various popular sports are depicted on the quilt, including tennis, archery and cricket.

All these motifs put together suggest the quilt aimed to take a humorous look at a leisured life in the British army in a far-flung post of the Empire. The cartoon caricatures of the soldiers, the Heavy and the Light Dragoon, definitely poke fun at the army. They are careful copies of cartoons by Thomas Seccombe, from *Army and Navy Drolleries*, published in England in the 1870s. Poems accompany Seccombe's original cartoons, and the one for the Heavy Dragoon reads:

Dragoon.

> *D stands for Dragoon; some called Heavy, some Light;*
> *To call this a heavy one surely is right.*
> *His bearskin informs us our friend is a Grey;*
> *So perhaps it would be only proper to say,*
> *Such a very big man on a charger so small,*
> *Is not drawn from nature, but what one might call*
> *A study in Greys, which some day may prove true*
> *When the British Dragoon has no hard work to do.*

No doubt whoever embroidered the Dragoon on the quilt was well aware of the poem that went with it, and wanted people to enjoy the message of a British army with 'no hard work to do'. The motifs on the quilt suggest that, rather than working, the army was enjoying playing cards, hunting ducks, and attending dances where ladies carried fans. They were also attending tea parties or were playing cricket, tennis or archery. Yet pride in the British Empire is all throughout the quilt, with the Prince of Wales Feathers, the mention of the Queen's Jubilee, and particularly in all the patriotic flags.

The oriental nature of many of the motifs seen in this quilt reflects the contemporary taste for all things Japanese, following the opening up of Japan to the West in the 1860s. The influence of the Japanese aesthetic is found throughout the arts and crafts of the late nineteenth century, and quilting was no exception.

A quilt from South Australia is also believed to be connected with the Jubilee celebrations in 1887. In that year, Adelaide's Exhibitions Building was formally opened as the site of the International Jubilee Exhibition. All kinds of items from all over the world were on display, but also included were woolwork, craftwork and needlework by people of South Australia.

Louisa Fanny Jury, who was born in Adelaide in 1841, only five years after the foundation of the colony of South Australia, married Jesse Catt in 1862. Jesse had arrived in Australia in 1849 and had worked at various jobs, including driving bullock teams, gold digging in Victoria, and as a stockman. The couple settled at Meadows, and Jesse worked as a mason, butcher and farmer. They had twelve children, and their oldest son, also called Jesse, became a draper and eventually went into a partnership in the drapery firm of Lloyd, Brook and Catt, a well-known firm in Port Adelaide for many years. Both Louisa and Jesse were devout members of their local Church of England at Meadows, and Jesse was a

MICHAL KLUVANEK

church warden, Sunday school superintendent and lay reader. Louisa made cushions and tapestry for the church, and church receipts account for the threads and fabrics used, some of them purchased from her son's firm. Jesse was civic-minded, and was prominent in local civic affairs, being a district councillor for twenty-five years, as well as being involved with other community and sporting activities. Louisa died in 1930.

To make her quilt, it would seem that Louisa used a patchwork pattern from *Caulfield's Dictionary of Needlework*, published in 1882. The exact same arrangement of squares and six-sided lozenge shapes in two sizes were given in *Caulfeild*, described as a 'pretty set pattern made with three different sized patches' and labelled as 'Mosaic Patchwork (No. 4)'. Louisa did not follow the shading suggested in *Caulfeild*, however, and also added her own touch by using darker colours to make a diamond at the centre of the quilt, then putting lighter fabrics around

the diamond which shade to darker colours at the quilt's edge. The quilt has been hand-pieced over papers, and is made of various silk fabrics, including brocades, printed silks, striped and checked taffeta and ribbed silks. Perhaps Louisa was able to obtain scraps from her son's drapery business. The quilt is machine-quilted, with cotton wadding as the inner layer, and backed with silk.

The family story attached to the quilt is that it was shown in a Jubilee exhibition. Research has not found Mrs Catt's name listed in any records or newspapers, but then most of the needlework was not described in detail. A beautiful silk pieced quilt would be a suitable and fashionable piece of needlework for a woman in Louisa Catt's position to have made. The quilt has been treasured by her descendants.

QUILT MADE BY LOUISA CATT *(above)*.
165 cm x 264 cm (65 in x 104 in). Collection Old Government House, Belair, South Australia.
CARTOON OF THE HEAVY DRAGOON *(left)*.

QUILT MADE BY CHRISTINA BROWN.
146 cm x 181 cm (57¹/₂ in x 71¹/₄ in).
Collection National Gallery of Australia, Canberra.

1890 TO 1900

QUILT MADE BY MARIANNE GIBSON. *218 cm x 225 cm*
(86 in x 89 in). Collection Wangaratta Historical Society, Victoria.

By the beginning of the 1890s, the Australian colonies had experienced a long boom time. Wealth had from come from gold and other mineral discoveries, and also from wool and later from wheat. The population had increased and, by the end of the century, both Sydney and Melbourne each had half a million people. The cities now had fine public and church buildings of stone and brick, built in grand neo-classic and neo-Gothic styles. A railway network made easier links between country and city, and also between city and city. Within cities, railways were allowing suburban development. The boom ended abruptly in the mid-1890s when speculation, especially in land, led to a bust, and a severe depression temporarily halted the expansion.

As for quilts, it would seem that this era was a golden age for quiltmaking, with all kinds of quilts being made all over Australia. In the 1890s, Australia participated in the taste for crazy patchwork which spread through the English-speaking world at this time. The early crazy quilts are extraordinary pieces of needlework. Not especially practical for bed-coverings, crazy quilts displayed the virtuosity of the maker with her needle. It was 'art for art's sake' expressed in quilts. Presumably, a crazy patchwork quilt also made a statement about the wealth and leisure of the maker, who showed that she had time to do decorative rather than useful sewing.

Christina Brown made a magnificent crazy quilt in the 1890s. Andrew Brown had settled in Australia in the 1820s. He married Christina Hendersen in 1841 when he was on a visit to Scotland. Coming to Australia, the couple lived on Andrew's large property called 'Cooerwull' at Bowenfels, near Lithgow, New South Wales. They had three children, but only their oldest son married and had a family. Andrew Brown was a wealthy man, but he was also a devout Presbyterian and civic-minded. He became a Justice of the Peace and a magistrate, and was a liberal benefactor to St Andrew's College of Sydney. He died in 1894. Christina, aged eighty, died in 1895.

The quilt is made of twelve large squares, each covered with odd shapes of silk or velvet. The edge of each patch is outlined with a variety of embroidery stitches, then beautifully embroidered motifs have been added to the patches. Mostly the motifs are flowers, such as lilies, roses, daisies, fuchsias, sunflowers – the flowers of England, not of Australia. There are also decorative embroidered initials, the most prominent being a large 'AB', presumably for Andrew Brown. Other embroidered motifs include butterflies, a teapot and Kate Greenaway-style figures of children.

DETAIL OF QUILT MADE BY MRS PATERSON (top). *Private collection.*
DETAIL OF QUILT MADE BY REBECCA KING (above). *Collection Art Gallery of South Australia, Adelaide.*

The 1890s was a time when Australia became more conscious of its own identity as a country rather than as a series of colonies. There was a growing push for the colonies to join together into a Federation. Conventions were held to discuss the constitutional issues involved, the first of which met in 1891 and another in 1897. It was a time of an emerging sense of nationalism, with an increased use of Australian symbols such as the wattle, the waratah, the kangaroo and the emu. These Australian motifs found their way into some quilts.

Marianne Gibson, of Wangaratta, Victoria, made her crazy quilt in the early 1890s and embroidered 1891 on one of the patches. Marianne was originally from Ireland, but came to Australia in 1837 and married Alexander Gibson in 1864. The Gibsons resided in the upstairs portion of their double-fronted store which sold general merchandise, hardware, and wine and spirits. Marianne's quilt is richly embroidered with all the typical motifs – the flowers, butterflies, fans, her initials and Kate Greenaway figures. She also added a portrait of a Japanese girl and flags of Britain, France and America. Consistent with the growing taste for Australian motifs, she embroidered a spray of the native Sturt's Desert Pea in the very centre of her quilt. Marianne also included some sprays of yellow wattle, and some red and green King parrots. The crazy patchwork blocks are divided by strips of ruched maroon silk, and the whole is framed by a wide border of maroon velvet with a zigzag edge which is further enhanced by a broad border of lace. The quilt is backed with honey-coloured silk which has been machine-quilted to a layer of padding. The story is told that Marianne's husband was asked how much the quilt cost, and he replied 'a pair of eyes'. Marianne had a family of five children and she died in 1911, aged seventy-four.

Other Australian crazy patchwork quilts of this era have

sprays of wattle worked into the patches, either using chenille thread or little woollen bobbles to make the flowers. Mrs Paterson, of Wedderburn in Victoria, made two crazy patchwork quilts, and she included wattle worked in chenille thread on some of the patches. A crazy quilt made in South Australia by Rebecca King, of Georgetown, has a wallaby and an emu on it, along with the usual teapots and butterflies. The quilt was made in 1895 as a wedding present for her sister.

One of the pleasures in creating crazy patchwork was the collection of the fabric pieces. Often these scraps were collected for sentimental reasons, such as those gathered by Marion Gibson (no relation to Marianne, above) for a crazy quilt she made around 1890 when she was living on a property called 'Narringa', near Hay. Marion Gemmel was born in Scotland, and had married John Gibson. Shortly after their marriage they sailed to Australia, arriving in Victoria. John worked as a bootmaker, but saved his money to buy land. In 1874, he selected land at Gunbar, near Hay. A devout Presbyterian, John helped found a church in the area. Marion and John had nine children – eight boys and one girl – though two boys died in infancy. John must have been proud of his wife's patchwork, as a family portrait shows him sitting with a crazy patchwork

QUILT MADE BY MARION GIBSON (top). 192 cm x 230 cm (76 in x 91 in). Collection Museum of Applied Arts and Sciences, Sydney. PORTRAIT OF JOHN AND MARION GIBSON (above).

cloth on the table in front of him.

When she was bequeathing the quilt to her grand-daughter, Marion wrote a letter about its making and what the quilt meant to her. She wrote of how 'it was all made with pieces from friends far and near. I called it the "Friendship quilt", and to me it was a labour of love'. The pieces of fabric in the quilt evoked memories of the givers, some coming from her family back in Scotland. There were pieces of wedding dresses from family and friends, baby ribbons, her own ribbons, pieces of dresses and neck-ties. 'Ties are well repre-sented' she wrote, 'one your Uncle Bob bought from Melbourne, and there is one of old Mr Budd, an early squatter. I put it beside one of your Grand-father's, so I went in for "Federation" on that "quilt" – for all classes are united'. So the national movement towards Federation was marked through a piece in Marion's crazy quilt. Marion embroidered her initials, and the date, 1892, in one corner. The quilt is backed with a cotton fabric which itself has a crazy patchwork pattern printed on it, and the edge is finished with a frill of lace.

Australian motifs are found on another intriguing quilt which is presumed to have been made in the late nine-teenth century. In the centre of the quilt, appliquéd in Turkey red, there is an emu

become the Commonwealth of Australia. Was the seven-pointed star an accident when the quiltmaker made her star pattern or was it deliberate? The seven-pointed stars were only added to the Australian flag in 1908, much later than this quilt is presumed to have been made. We do not know, as little is known about the maker of the quilt, except that it is attributed to a Mrs Brown of Bowning, New South Wales.

and a kangaroo on either side of a shield or crown shape. Each animal looks backwards over its shoulder, a pose that is found in many unofficial Australian coats of arms throughout the nineteenth century. It is an image with long antecedents. The very first picture of a kangaroo, which was sent back to Europe from Captain Cook's expedition, showed the animal looking backwards over its shoulder, and the image persisted for well over a century. The kangaroo and emu as a coat of arms were first painted onto a patriotic flag made by the Bowman family in 1806, after they received news of Nelson's victory at Trafalgar. The coat of arms in the centre of the quilt is surrounded by four stars, and another four stars are in the corners of the second row of piecing beyond the centre. Each star has seven points, which is interesting because the seven-pointed star was adopted for the stars (except the smallest star of the Southern Cross) on the official Australian flag after Federation. The large seven-pointed star on the flag represents the six states and the Federal Territories that united in Federation to

The quilt was owned by Margaret Swan, whose family came to live at Elizabeth Farm, the old Macarthur homestead, in the early 1900s. Margaret Swan was a keen collector of Australiana and spent holidays at Bowning.

The quilt is pieced of squares and triangles, and has been made in the medallion style. The piecing is crude, the materials are humble cottons, and some of the patches are themselves extensively patched. The back of the quilt is made of small patches of white fabric sewn together in the most frugal way. The patchwork top and backing have been flat-quilted together and a heart has been quilted in the centre of the red shield shape.

In 1899, when Britain declared war on the Boers in South Africa, Australia enthusiastically offered to help by sending soldiers. Australians were then involved in the war which dragged on until 1902. A small quilt is connected to Australia's involvement in the war. Typical of quilts made by soldiers from woollen uniform fabrics in the late nineteenth century, it has over seven thousand pieces sewn into an intricate geometric pattern, and is attributed to Millist Vincent, of Tasmania. This kind of patchwork may not have been unusual in Australia. Kate Rodd wrote reminiscences about her grandmother's house in Hobart, Tasmania, as the house was, just after the turn of the century. Over the couch in the 'back room' was 'a patchwork cover made of small squares, red, white and blue scraps from the makings of the dress

uniforms of the officers in the South African War'.

The English pieced-over-papers method persisted, especially quilts of hexagons. Sophia Wilbow made many quilts, as she had fourteen children, eight of them girls. She determined to make each of her daughters a quilt and three of the quilts survive. Sophia's husband, Thomas Mitchell, was a farmer and hotel owner in the Windsor area of New South Wales. He died in 1896 after a long illness, and the family recall that Sophia sewed patchwork during the long hours spent sitting at his bedside. Sophia made her quilts from scraps of cotton fabric and lined them with attractive printed cotton fabrics which must have been specially purchased for the quilts. Amongst Sophia's possessions at her death was a copy of a little booklet on patchwork taken from *Caulfeild's Dictionary of Needlework*, so this may have been a source of information about patchwork.

Many Log Cabin quilts date from around the turn of the century, and unlike the crazy patchwork confections of silk and velvet, they are usually made of scraps left over from everyday clothing. Mrs Hannah Rhodes, of Hindmarsh in South Australia, made a quilt in which the Log Cabin blocks are sewn into groups of fours so that crosses are formed at the

SOPHIA WILBOW (above).
QUILT MADE BY SOPHIA WILBOW (right).
188 cm x 204 cm (74 in x 80 in).
Collection National Gallery of Australia, Canberra.
COAT OF ARMS QUILT (far left), attributed to
Mrs Brown. 128 cm x 203 cm (50 in x 80 in).
Collection Museum of Applied Arts and Sciences, Sydney.
QUILT MADE BY MILLIST VINCENT (left).
124 cm x 126 cm (49 in x 50 in). Private collection.

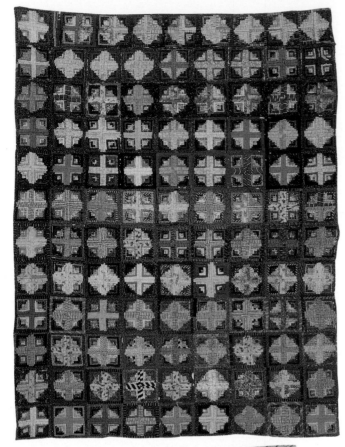

STEVE STRIKE

centres of each four. The strips in the quilt are very narrow, many only 6 mm ($1/4$ in) to 12 mm ($1/2$ in) wide, and each block is only about 10 cm (4 in) in size. All kinds of fabrics have been used, including cotton prints, woollen fabrics, flannelette and furnishing fabrics. A grand-daughter could later recall that some of the pieces came from their grandfather's trousers and shirts. The quilt is lined with maroon sateen, and lines of stitching attach the layers together, although the stitching does not go through all the layers in all places.

The Smith sisters made a Log Cabin quilt around the turn of the century. The Smith family lived at Woodgrove, near Hall, in New South Wales (now part of the Australian Capital Territory). There were five sisters in the family, several of them dressmakers. Their mother, Jane Smith, returned from an outing one day with the idea of how to make a quilt from a design she had seen. She set the girls to cutting up scraps left over from their dressmaking and sewing the pieces together on the machine. In the 1980s, Elvena, one of the sisters, could recall where many of the fabrics in the quilt had come from. One fabric she herself had worn on an outing to the Yarrongabilly caves. She recalled that the girls did not understand how the squares they sewed would eventually go together, but their mother laid them out to make the final design. The quilt was finished with a furnishing fabric bought specially to make the backing, and a frill was added around three sides. The quilt became the property of Beatrice, and was used for many years.

In Carlston, Victoria, Nicholes Wallace made a large Log Cabin quilt. Nicholes Brown, a widow, was the second wife of Isaac Wallace, a farmer in the area. She made quilts for all her daughters-in-law, and the one pictured was made for John Brown, one of her four sons by her first marriage, who married Alma Gibbs in 1902. It is believed that the quilt was made around 1895. In this Log Cabin quilt the starting square was put in the corner of the block rather than the centre, with strips of dark and light fabrics building up the remainder of the block. The quilt is finished with a wonderful border of alternating dark and light wedge shapes, then a

BICA PHOTOGRAPHICS

QUILT MADE BY THE SMITH SISTERS (above).
182 cm x 208 cm (72 in x 82 in). Private collection.
SMITH SISTERS (right).
QUILT MADE BY HANNAH RHODES (top left).
166 cm x 231 cm (65 in x 91 in). Private collection.
QUILT MADE BY NICHOLES WALLACE (bottom left).
234 cm x 236 cm (92 in x 93 in). Collection National Pioneer
Women's Hall of Fame, Alice Springs.

KEN STEPNELL

KEN STEPNELL

wide binding at the edge. The quilt has no backing and, unusual for the time, was not pieced onto a foundation.

Two appliquéd quilts made in Australia around 1900 are unusual in that they have a repeating block design which is typical of American appliqué, but not at all like any other Australian quilts of this period. That the two quilts used essentially the same design and were made by friends living in the same area, Portland, Victoria, suggests there must have been a common source. Miss Lydia Liddle, who had a shop in Portland, made one quilt. Little is known about Lydia Liddle, other than that she was an excellent needlewoman. The quilt was given to a friend, and handed down and cherished within the friend's family. The quilt is beautifully stitched and quilted. The floral blocks, which have a red bell-shaped flower design, are placed on point, with a marvellous meandering vine of further flowers and leaves around the edge. Miss Liddle elaborately embroidered her initials in red thread in the centre of the quilt. The quilt is quilted in a pattern of clam shells with sunflowers in the alternate plain blocks.

Nearby in Condah, Arrabella Cannon made her version of the same quilt. In her quilt, she arranged the leaves on the stem slightly differently, placed

QUILT MADE BY LYDIA LIDDLE *(top left).*
201 cm x 206 cm (78 in x 81 in). Private collection.
APPLIQUE QUILT MADE BY ARRABELLA CANNON
(left). 214 cm x 275 cm (84 in x 108 in). Private collection.

44

the blocks together in a straight set, and made the meandering border a little less elaborate. The green originally used for the stems and leaves has now faded to mole brown. The quilt is quilted with a pattern of squares with flowers and leaves in the alternate blocks. Arrabella Armstrong was born in Ireland and came to Australia in 1856. She married William Cannon and they lived at Prospect Vale, in Condah. They had six children, two sons and four daughters. As only one daughter married, Arrabella had daughters at home to help her, leaving her free to pursue her patchwork. Arrabella Cannon died in 1912. Besides the appliquéd quilt, she also made three Log Cabin quilts, one of which was left unfinished. Arrabella used just two fabrics, a light and a dark, to make her Log Cabin blocks in the arrangement known as Courthouse Steps. This gives a pattern of triangles all over the quilt, and as she set the blocks on point, the quilt has a zigzag edge.

Charlotte Gambold, of the Wangaratta district, made her quilt in the medallion style. Made from cotton fabrics, and sewn mostly by hand, it is also backed with cotton. It is not known precisely when she made the quilt, but it may have been for the wedding of her sister Elizabeth to Mr A.H. Bennett of Everton Upper, in 1893. The quilt has been handed down through Elizabeth's family. Charlotte made several quilts, as family members recall other ones she made for them, but these have long since worn out. Charlotte lived in the Wangaratta district from when she was about six years old, the oldest child of three in the family of Thorres and Mary Gambold who settled in the area in 1866. A devout Methodist, she taught Sunday school and walked the 4 miles (6.5 kilometres) from her home to the church many, many times. Charlotte was also a keen shooter, and was a member of the Everton rifle club. Her scrapbooks contain cuttings which interested her, and she especially collected articles on sporting feats.

LOG CABIN QUILT MADE BY ARRABELLA CANNON *(top right)*. *203 cm x 238 cm (80 in x 94 in). Private collection.*
QUILT MADE BY CHARLOTTE GAMBOLD *(right)*.
210 cm x 240 cm (83 in x 94 in). Private collection.

QUILT MADE BY THE HAMPSON SISTERS.
200 cm x 300 cm (79 in x 118 in).
Collection National Gallery of Australia, Canberra.

1901 TO 1913

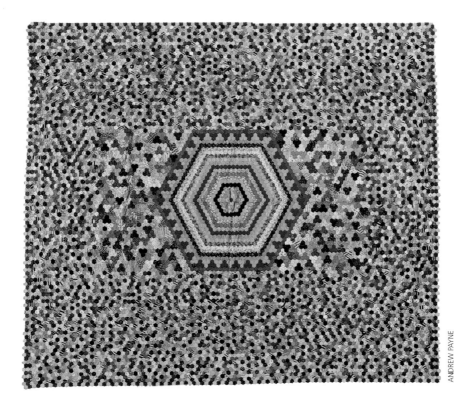

ANDREW PAYNE

QUILT MADE BY RICHARD WILLIAMS.
191 cm x 216 cm (75 in x 85 in). Private collection.

On 1 January 1901, the colonies became states and united to become the Commonwealth of Australia. After a decade of discussions and negotiations, Federation had been finally agreed to and the necessary act passed by the British Parliament. Australia adopted a British Westminster system for the election of the House of Representatives, the lower house, and followed the American states-rights model for the Senate, the upper house.

Even though Australia as a country came into existence with Federation, Australians were still British subjects, and saw themselves very much as part of the great British Empire. Loyalty to Britain remained high, and these attitudes of loyalty to the Queen and the Empire are expressed in a quilt made by the Hampson sisters of Westbury, Tasmania. The quilt is made of squares of Turkey-red fabric, embroidered with white thread, a reversal of the usual red embroidery on white. Queen Victoria is proudly placed in the centre of the quilt underneath the words 'Victoria the Good 1900'. Other patriotic sentiments on the quilt are shown in a square which proclaims 'Rule Britannia Rule the Waves' and another with a lion saying 'Oh the British lion is a noble scion' and ending with the warning to 'beware how you tread on his tail'. The virtues of 'Faith', 'Hope' and 'Charity' are embroidered large, as are other little homilies, such as 'Work is the best antidote to worry', 'Lost time is never found again', and 'Could everything be done twice everything would be done better'. Some of the advice is humorous, such as 'When a woman throws herself at a man's head she seldom hits the mark'. Some of the advice seems contradictory, as one square reads 'One man may lead another to drink but fifty cant keep him from it', while another says 'Eat drink and

47

be merry'. The teapot is shown as 'A faithful friend'. Throughout the quilt there are images of animals, all given names, such as Boz the dog, Polly and Kitty the cows, and Bobs the kangaroo. There are houses and cottages shown, and the shop of Mr Drew in Westbury. The quilt may have been made for a raffle, as one square says 'Good luck to the winner of this'. There are dates embroidered on the quilt, from 1900 in the centre to 1903 in an outer square. Perhaps by the time the quilt was finished it was too old-fashioned for its purpose, Queen Victoria having died in 1901, only weeks after the Federation of Australia was declared.

Little is known about the makers of the quilt. One of the Misses Fitzpatrick purchased the quilt 'from the milkman' some fifty years ago, and for many years it hung in their hotel, Fitzpatrick's Inn, in Westbury. Research indicates that the Hampson family lived at Fern Bank, near Westbury, and in 1903, the electoral roll shows that there were five daughters living with their parents – Mary, Hannah, Isabella, Evangeline and Jane. The quilt was purchased from the brother-in-law of the sisters, but may have come via a neighbour, Bert Gray, who used to make deliveries to the Fitzpatrick's Inn.

As well as fund-raising, a major reason for making quilts was usually family use. In Sydney, Richard Crofts Williams, inactive because of sciatica, spent his time stitching patchwork and made seven patchwork quilts, one for each of his children when they married, and one to raise money for his church. Richard Williams was a staunch Methodist, and the quilt he made for the church was the subject of a game to guess how many pieces there were in it. Richard died in 1921, aged eighty-seven years. One quilt which survives was made in 1912 for the marriage of one of his daughters, the last of the family to marry. It is made of cotton fabrics and consists of

very small 13 mm ($^{1}/_{2}$ in) hexagons, all neatly stitched in a pattern that radiates out from the centre.

Margery Harvey, of the Bathurst area, New South Wales, made quilts until she died in 1909, aged ninety-two. In a letter to one of her daughters that her descendants believe Margery wrote just several months before she died, she mentions sending a quilt for the children, presumed to be her great-grandchildren born in 1907 and 1909. She wrote that she had been sent '10s to get the linen so I got lining and wadding and made a print quilt that will do for the children[s] bed and stand washing … me and Elizabeth quilted it after a fashion the past fortnight but with a lot of pain[,] my head and neck have been very bad with neuralgia'. It is not known when she made one of her two surviving quilts, but in 1938, the Bathurst home of two of her daughters was described in an article in the *Sunday Sun and Guardian*. The article said 'Indoors every bed is covered by a brilliantly colored patchwork quilt, stitched with the most delicate embroidery … the quilts are miracles of industry and patience. Every little scrap of material has its history.' The sisters could recall which were scraps from their mother's wedding dress and another dress their mother wore the day that one of

QUILT MADE BY MARGERY HARVEY. *173 cm x 176 cm (68 in x 69 in). Private collection.*

QUILT MADE BY SARAH MARSHALL *(above). Courtesy National Parks and Wildlife Service, New South Wales.*
CRAZY PATCHWORK QUILT FROM MELBOURNE *(right). 164 cm x 228 cm (65 in x 90 in). Private collection.*

panic and kept on scalding the milk in a saucepan. The sight of her doing this touched the bushranger, as it reminded him of his mother in England, and he promised not to harm her and accepted her offer of a drink of milk and some scones. Margery and Edmund had eleven children, and the couple eventually settled in the Oberon area, near Bathurst. Margery wrote in her reminiscences of the isolation many Australian pioneer women experience. 'I was there quite six months and never saw another woman.'

Margery Harvey's quilt is made from a variety of fabrics, including wool, and is padded with wadding and quilted in black thread. The central star is pieced, and the other stars have been pieced and appliquéd into place. The remnants of papers can be seen behind some of the patches, and there are also some remnants of appliqué still remaining. Embroidery in wool embellishes the edges of the piecing and there are vestiges of embroidery left on the inner border.

Like many of the women who made quilts, Sarah Marshall made a lot of them. Her grandson, Charles, recalled her sitting in the dining room, holding court, with the Bible on one side of her chair and her sewing box on the other.

In 1856, Sarah Langslow Adams had married James Marshall, a man who had been to California in the goldrush of 1848, then came to Australia to do mining in the Sofala area in New South Wales. They had eleven children and, in 1875, James built a large house at Hill End. Sarah died in 1926, aged ninety. The family kept the house as it always had been, with Sarah's patchwork quilts on all the beds, with plenty to spare to drape over chairs and chests. Several of the old iron beds still have lovely lace testers hanging above them and old-fashioned wash-stands nearby.

Sarah's quilts were thrifty quilts. She used whatever materials were on hand to make them, whether wool or cotton, and she put the pieces together in

them fell off her pony. The photo accompanying the article shows the two women in front of a star quilt very like the one shown on the previous page.

Margery Taylor had married Edmund Harvey in Cornwall in 1837. Four days later they left for Australia. The couple brought the money Edmund had inherited, but the money dwindled away as bad luck followed them through drought, fire, and even encounters with bushrangers. The family stories of bushrangers were reported in the *Bathurst Times* in 1935. While at Orange, Edmund was robbed by Lowry, Fireball and Thunderbolt, who crept up to his tent, held him up with his own gun, and stole his money, clothing and effects — even taking his beautiful beaver skin hat and substituting a dirty cabbage tree hat. Edmund protested vainly that 'they might leave a man his hat'. On another occasion, Margery was confronted with a bushranger, but she did not whatever style suited the patches – simple pieced shapes, crazy patchwork, or some combination of both. Even the backs of her quilts were patched using larger pieces of fabric.

Crazy patchwork continued to be in vogue in the early twentieth century. One quilt makes a small

Melbourne, although nothing is known about the maker. The quilt is constructed in blocks, and is an odd shape in that it has three corners missing and has a fringe around only some of the sides. Perhaps it was a table cover that someone was later converting into a quilt, but did not finish. The

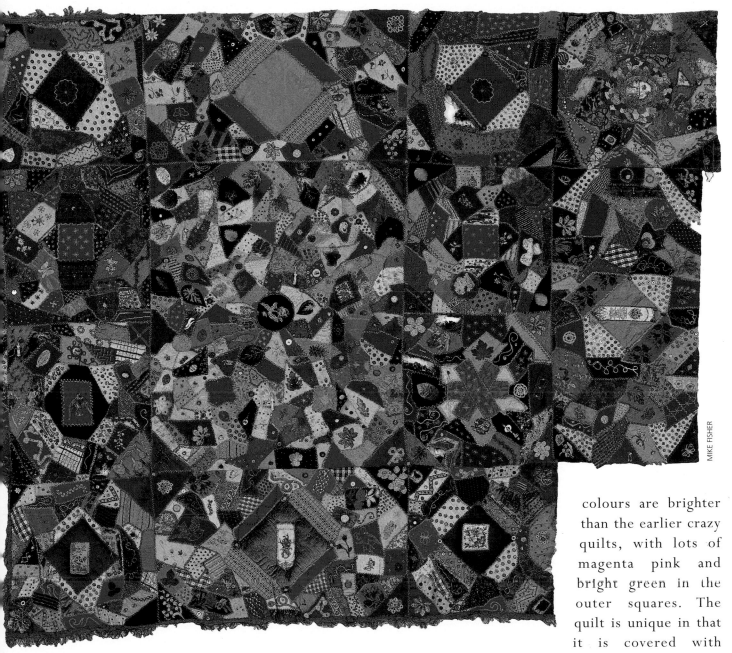

MIKE FISHER

colours are brighter than the earlier crazy quilts, with lots of magenta pink and bright green in the outer squares. The quilt is unique in that it is covered with

reference to the Australian love of cricket, the summer game which came with the English settlers. It also mentions another important theme in Australian life – the unions which care for the welfare of the workers. The quilt is a large piece of crazy patchwork and was probably made in

beads, buttons, brooches, buckles and badges. There are sequins and ribbons, some of them with pictures on them, such as one of Little Red Riding Hood. Another ribbon celebrates the achievement of the eight-hour day by the Shop Assistants' Union. The three 8s on the ribbon represent the worker's ideal of 8 hours of labour, 8 hours of recreation and 8 hours of rest, a goal achieved after hard work by the unions. 'God is Love' proclaims one ribbon, and 'Birthday Greeting' another. One small snippet of ribbon, which has been carefully stitched around, says 'To Dear One', and there are several little buttons of photographs, one a portrait of a beautiful young girl. One little copper badge has ER VII on it, obviously a reference to King Edward VII who came to the throne after Queen Victoria. Among the many badges, there is one for the prestigious Melbourne Cricket Club, 1903–4 season. This crazy patchwork must have had lots of personal meaning for the maker, but its stories and meaning remain hidden as we have no clues about who she was.

Another unique crazy quilt, also made in Melbourne, was created by Margaret Weir. Margaret was born in Steiglitz, in Victoria, in 1856. The family later moved to Melbourne, probably after the death of Margaret's father in 1882. Margaret did not marry, although an earnest young missionary did make an offer. The family story tells that her suitor, perhaps unaccustomed to city noises, was awoken in the night by the toot of a train. He leaped out of bed thinking it was the last trumpet and called, 'Yes Lord, I'm ready'.

In 1890 and 1891, Margaret studied drawing in courses at the School of Design of the National Gallery Art School. Later she taught drawing and

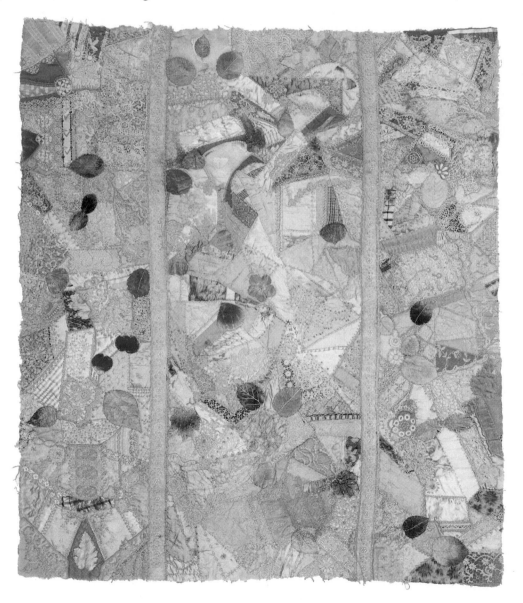

painting privately, and in the late 1920s she had an exhibition of her paintings of Australian wild flowers, although none sold. Margaret died in 1934.

Made of pieces of silks and velvets like other crazy patchwork, Margaret's quilt is different in that it is softer and more pastel in colour. It is covered with pieces of cream lace and has two bands of lace across the quilt. Embroidery in gold-coloured thread has been worked over the surface of the quilt, with the stitches going through a layer of padding behind the patchwork. Although the patchwork was finished and a lining was bought, the lining was never attached. It was probably made early in the twentieth century, as relatives recalled that it was displayed to them in the 1920s.

While early Suffolk Puff quilts were generally made from all-white fabrics, later ones are made of print fabrics. Olive Bibb made a large Suffolk Puff quilt from all kinds of cotton fabrics, although it is believed that the quilt was once bigger than it is now. Olive was a young widow with six children when, in 1917, she married John Bibb, the architect who designed the Congregational Chapel in Pitt Street and the Chapel for Seaman at the Rocks, both in central Sydney. Olive had three more children before she tragically died of blood poisoning when she was expecting her tenth child in 1923. The quilt was probably made sometime before her second marriage. Both Olive and her mother enjoyed doing patchwork, and one of her daughters remembered her sewing such things early in the century. The cotton fabrics she used may have been samples as some of them come in several different colourways.

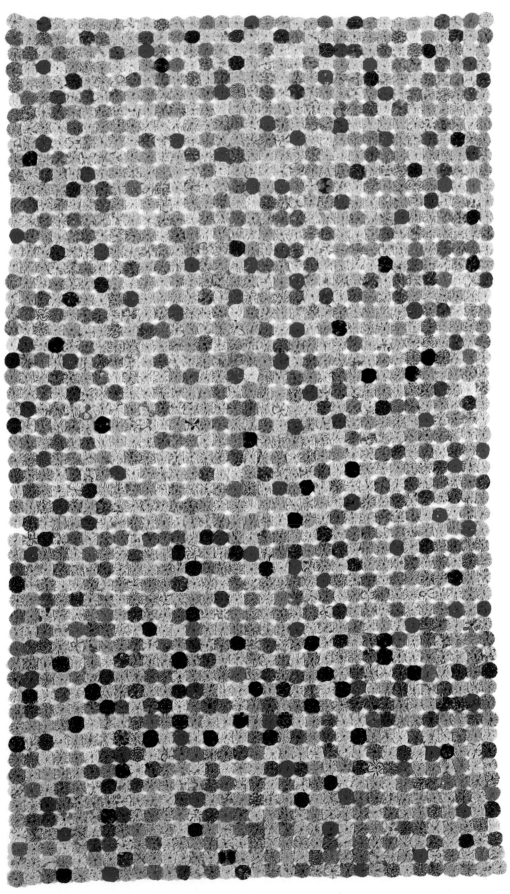

CRAZY PATCHWORK BY MARGARET WEIR *(left)*.
102 cm x 117 cm (40 in x 46 in).
Collection National Gallery of Australia, Canberra.
QUILT MADE BY OLIVE BIBB *(right). 104 cm x 183 cm (41 in x 72 in). Private collection.*

ANDREW PAYNE

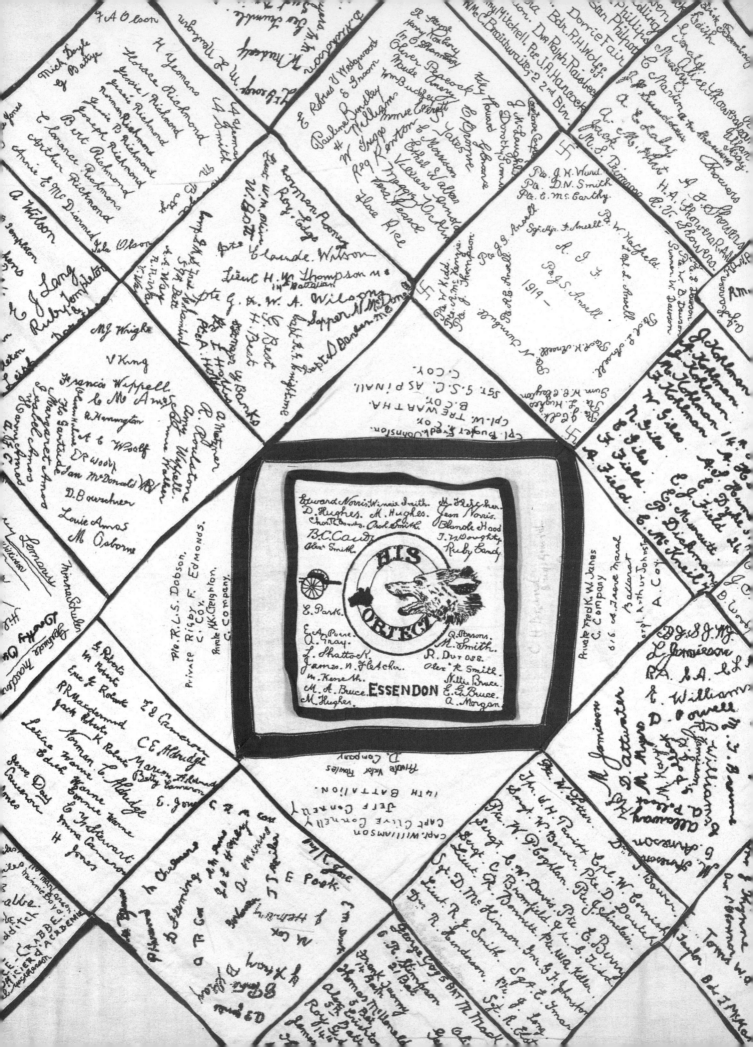

1914 TO 1918

CAPTAIN HANSEN.

On 4 August 1914, Britain declared war on Germany and automatically, as part of the Empire, Australia was also at war. Even before the war had begun, Mr Fisher of the Labor party was promising that 'Australians will stand beside our own to help and defend her to our last man and last shilling'. Although a minority opposed the war, the general reaction to the war was reflected in the words of the popular song 'Australia will be there'. Men rushed to enlist, and by early 1915, the first Australian Infantry Forces, the AIF, had left Australia. Based on a plan of Winston Churchill, then First Lord of the Admiralty, Britain had decided to attack Turkey, an ally of Germany, in the Dardanelles. For this attack, Australian and New Zealand soldiers were combined into the Australian and New Zealand Army Corps, the ANZACs. On 25 April 1915, Australian soldiers landed on the beaches of Gallipoli and fought the Turks in the steep and rugged hills. Stubborn resistance by the Turks eventually resulted in a stalemate, and in December, the British forces withdrew, concealing their retreat with guns ingeniously set up to fire after they had left. While not a military success, the bravery and courage shown by the soldiers created the 'Anzac tradition' honoured by Australians ever since.

In 1916 Australian soldiers were sent to France, where they, like millions of soldiers from both sides of the war, fought in the mud and horror of the bloody battlefields of France and Belgium.

Stewart Murray Hansen, a young architect from Williamstown, Victoria, was among the men who enlisted in September 1914. He joined the 14th battalion of the AIF and became a sergeant. In 1915 he was in the landing and fighting at Gallipoli. In 1916 he was sent to France, and in August he was awarded the Military Cross because of his action in the battle at Pozières. The citation reads:

Initiative and devotion to duty in carrying out orders. Pushing forward at Strong point 77. On 27/28th/16 his Coy attacked the enemy strong points 54 and 27 and it was due to him positions were gained and consolidation commenced before having to withdraw owing to counter attack in large numbers. Remained after Coy relieved to pass on full instructions. Previously recommended for work on Gallipoli and at Bois Grenier.

The battle at Pozières was one of the big and costly actions with which the AIF was involved. Altogether, it lost 23 000 officers and men, half of the four divisions' fighting strength. C.E.W. Bean, the Australian official historian of the war, wrote that one of the ridges where the battle was fought was 'more densely sown with Australian sacrifice than any other place on earth'.

Throughout all his service, Captain Hansen was collecting signatures for a quilt which his mother was making. He asked people with whom he came into contact to sign cotton squares supplied by his mother. The squares were then sent back to Australia, and were embroidered in red by his mother, his aunt and other mothers and friends of the 14th Battalion. Food parcels were sent to the troops wrapped in calico, so this was the probable source of the squares of cloth.

The quilt commemorates important action by the 14th Battalion, including the heroism of its most famous member, Albert Jacka. He also enlisted in September 1914, and saw action at Gallipoli where he was awarded the Victoria Cross, the highest award for bravery in action. In an attack on an Australian position, Turkish bombs had cleared a bay of the Australian trenches and nine Turks entered it. Jacka single-handedly leapt into the bay, and, while his mates held the enemy's attention, he killed six and wounded and captured one. Later in France,

Jacka also was awarded the Military Cross for action at Pozières, and a bar was added for action at Bullecourt in 1917. There were two other recommendations for Albert Jacka, although no award was given.

A square of the quilt commemorates Jacka's action at Gallipoli. Under an embroidered Australian army badge of the Rising Sun, a description of the VC award is briefly given:

14th Battalion A.I.F. 1st Australian V.C. May 19th 1915 5 a.m. Lance Corporal Albert Jacka. Wedderburn. Recommended for distinction by Lieut. Wallace-Crabbe. Party also engaged in V.C. incident Lieut. Hamilton. L/Cpl De Arango. Lieut. Boyle. Pte. Poliness.

Although wounded several times and gassed, Albert Jacka returned to Australia after the war. Tragically, Captain Stewart Hansen was mortally wounded at the battle of Gueudecourt on 4 February 1917, and died on 7 February, his twenty-fifth birthday. The battle had gained some six hundred yards (six hundred metres), but at a cost of seven officers and two hundred and twenty-six men of the 13th Battalion, and a company of the 14th Battalion lost ninety-five of one hundred and twenty men.

Captain Hansen's mother and friends continued to make the quilt which bears dates of 1918 and 1919. All the cream squares, with their embroidered names of soldiers and nurses, were edged with red, then assembled together on point, with five squares centred into spaces created at the centre and in each corner.

While men could enlist, what could women do? As soon as war was declared, Red Cross groups began to form all over Australia. By the end of the war, some two thousand two hundred branches had been established and the Red Cross Depot in Melbourne had sent out 320 389 pyjamas, 457 311 shirts, 1 163 049 pairs of socks, 142 708

QUILT MADE BY MRS HANSEN AND FRIENDS. *165 cm x 225 cm (66 in x 90 in). Collection Williamstown Historical Society, Victoria.*

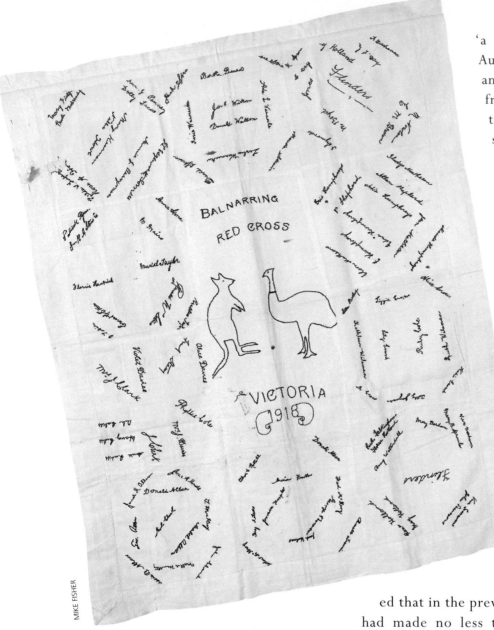

MIKE FISHER

'a casualty list of 9,000 for Australia and one or two deaths and several wounded in the men from our own immediate location, the awful horrors of war should be apparent to us all. If these stricken men have seen their duty and have gone to face it in spite of wounds and death, how much more should we – whose safety and sanctity they are guaranteeing – how much more should we bend earnestly to the work of doing our much smaller duty of providing these patriots with those necessities and comforts they so sorely need.'

News from Gallipoli was reaching home.

Beside knitting socks, the women made clothes and many other items for the soldiers, including quilts. On 5 January 1917, the *Peninsula Post* reported that in the previous year the Balnarring branch had made no less than '37 pillows, 211 pairs of socks, 239 shirts, 19 scarves, 5 knotted slippers, 2 pair bedsocks, 9 quilts, 5 cholera belts, 5 Balaclava helmets, 73 pillow cases, 71 sheets, 43 bags, 12 sugar bags, 13 pyjamas, 26 face washers and various parcels of linen and bandages'.

In 1918, members of the Balnarring branch made a quilt. Typical of quilts made to raise money for the Red Cross, it is made of squares of white

mufflers, 8307 mittens and 3000 cases of old linen. Money was also raised to buy cigarettes, tobacco, pipes, toothbrushes and tins of cocoa, coffee and milk. The Australian Comforts Fund was established in 1916 to help soldiers and their families in Australia, and also to send food, clothing and comforts overseas. Previous 'fancy work for dainty fingers' gave way to 'useful work for anxious fingers'.

The little community at Balnarring, of the Mornington Peninsula in Victoria, was a typical example. A Red Cross group formed immediately after war was declared. By 2 July 1915, the call was urgent and the *Peninsula Post* reported that with

QUILT MADE BY BALNARRING RED CROSS *(top)*. *87 cm x 112 cm (34 in x 44 in). Collection Red Cross Society, Victorian Division.*
QUILT MADE BY ROMSEY DISTRICT RED CROSS *(right). 150 cm x 190 cm (59 in x 75 in). Collection Red Cross Society, Victorian Division.*

MIKE FISHER

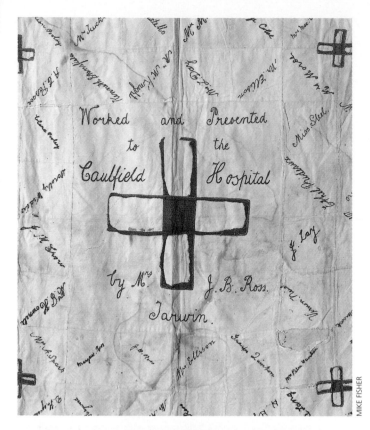

MIKE FISHER

DETAIL OF QUILT MADE BY JULIA ROSS *(top)*.
Collection Red Cross Society, Victorian Division.
MRS JULIA ROSS *(above)*.

cotton fabric with embroidered signatures in red thread. In the centre are an emu and a kangaroo, and in large letters 'Balnarring Red Cross' and 'Victoria 1918'. The signatures reflect the names of people who made donations to have their names included. Sometimes people paid for other people's names to be included, and this is how Phyllis Cole's name was included, as she was only a very small child at the time. Her mother was very active in the Red Cross, and no doubt had included her daughter's name. Many names from the district are found on the quilt, such as names from the Stone and Warnecke families. Two young men of the Stone family enlisted and were welcomed home in 1919. Private Warnecke was not so fortunate, and his death was announced in the paper in November 1917.

The Romsey district, north of Melbourne, made a fine patriotic Red Cross quilt with large red crosses decorating each corner and a British flag taking pride of place in the centre. The Australian flag is also there, but it is below the British flag and only in outline, not full colour. Inspirational texts are embroidered large at top and bottom, and little messages are dotted around the quilt, such as 'Honour the King', 'To thine own self be true', 'Seek ye the Lord', 'Onward and upward' and 'For Australia'. Included among the signatures are those of some soldiers.

Mrs Julia Ross, who lived at Tarwin in the Gippsland district of Victoria, made a quilt for the Meeniyan Red Cross. Again, the quilt is typical of signature quilts, with red embroidered signatures on cream squares. The *Leongatha Great Southern Star* reported on 27 July 1918 that 'Mrs Ross's autograph quilt ... raised £6/1/6d at 6d per name'. She received a certificate from the Red Cross for being 'one of five workers doing the largest amount of work during the year to 4 August'. Julia Ross had a special interest in the war, as three of her four sons enlisted. Frank Ross joined up in 1914 and served at Gallipoli and Egypt. Ewen Ross was wounded at Gallipoli and also in France. He was taken prisoner at Bullecourt in April 1917, and was a prisoner for the rest of the war. The Red

Cross was vital for Julia's communication to her POW son, and was the means by which she sent him money and letters. Her youngest son, Roy, enlisted in 1915 when he turned twenty-one. He was killed at Fromelles, France, less than a year later. The attack at Fromelles was the AIF's first great battle on the Western Front. It was a terrible disaster in which the Australian 5th Division lost five thousand five hundred and thirty-three men, including four hundred who were taken prisoner.

The virtue of patriotism had always been taught in Australia's schools, but the coming of the war encouraged this even further, especially in the state schools and the Protestant private schools. Flags, especially the British Union Jack, were waved and older boys did weekly drills of marching, standing to attention and saluting. In Victoria, the Caulfield Military Hospital was adopted by state school children as a focus for their war endeavours. Schools were rostered to provide comforts on a weekly basis. Balnarring School, for instance, was rostered for the first week of July 1916.

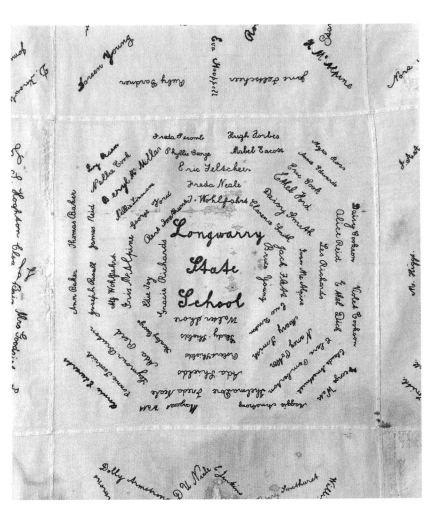

DETAIL OF LONGWARRY STATE SCHOOL QUILT.
Collection Red Cross Society, Victorian Division.

Some children made quilts, such as the children of Errol Street School in Melbourne who made a Patriotic Quilt in 1918, collecting a total of £7 for the names embroidered on it. The children presented the quilt to the soldiers, along with gifts of foodstuffs and a concert. Longwarry is a small town east of Melbourne, in Victoria, and the children of Longwarry School also made a signature quilt. The signatures are arranged into patterns and the school's name is embroidered in the centre of the quilt. The quilt is edged with a border of red cotton twill.

One of the names at the centre of the quilt is Eric Bruton. There were ten children in the Bruton family, and Eric, born in 1906, was the second youngest. He had six older brothers, and Allan, Lyster, Roland and Vernon all joined up. Allan

served in Gallipoli and France. Lyster served in Gallipoli, the Middle East and in France, and was killed in France in January 1917. Roland enlisted in January 1918, and served in France. Vernon joined up in August 1918, but the war ended before he could be sent overseas. Lyster, Allan and Roland Bruton are amongst the many names on the school Honour Roll which is a dark wooden plaque with gold lettering, a plaque typical of many such rolls erected in schools and churches.

Altogether, 416 809 Australians enlisted, and 331 781 of these were sent overseas. Of these, 59 342 were killed and more than 152 171 were wounded, giving Australia one of the highest casualty rates of the war. The Great War, as it was then called, bit deeply into the lives and psyches of Australians.

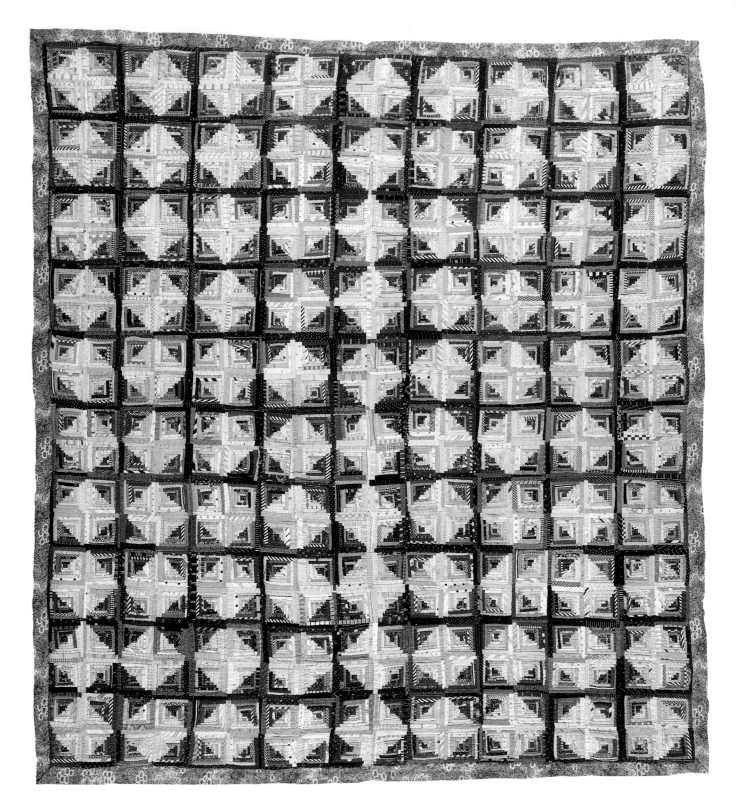

QUILT MADE BY SARAH MONUMENT. *142 cm x 155 cm (56 in x 61 in).*
Collection National Gallery of Australia, Canberra.

1919 TO 1938

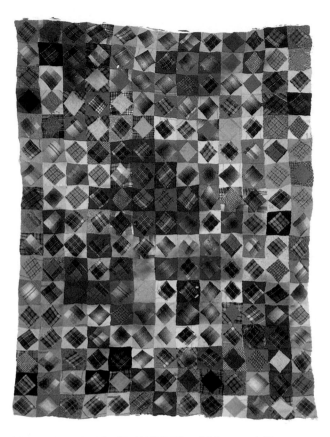

QUILT MADE BY ALICE FARRER. *183 cm x 140 cm*
(72 in x 55 in). Collection National Gallery of Australia, Canberra.

The years after the First World War proved more difficult than the returning soldiers, the diggers, expected. Many soldiers returned with broken health and lifelong disabilities. Soldier settlement was a plan to have the men take up small farms in the country, but over half the farms failed because of the inexperience of the soldiers, the small size of the farms, the lack of capital, and the ever-present threats of the Australian bush — drought and fire. Yet the new nation flourished in many ways. Canberra was established as the nation's capital and Parliament House was opened by the Duke of York in 1927. The cities expanded as more and more people took up the Australian suburban ideal of a detached house on its own plot of land. Technology increasingly impacted on everyday lives as houses were connected to electricity and as radio was introduced into homes.

In 1929, the stock market crashed in New York, precipitating the Great Depression worldwide. Australia suffered harshly and, at the worst time in the early 1930s, almost one-third of men were out of work. The whole economy spiralled downwards and the government cut wages and pensions. For many it was a time of 'make do and mend', not just because of thrift, but for sheer survival. However, the more well-to-do, those with secure jobs or large acres of good land, did not suffer to the extent that the families of the unemployed or the farmers on marginal land did.

The primary role for most women continued to be domestic work in the home. Patchwork was pursued because of its potential double role in 'making something from nothing' by using scraps and the creation of something to make a home more beautiful.

QUILT MADE BY MARY JANE HANNAFORD.
168 cm x 190 cm (66 in x 74³/4 in).
Collection National Gallery of Australia, Canberra.

Sarah Monument used tiny scraps to make her Log Cabin quilt. Sarah made the quilt over eighteen years, using bits of fabric which were very narrow, as the strips measure only about 6 mm (¹/4 in) in the finished quilt. Typical of most Log Cabin quilts, all kinds of fabrics were used, including cotton, linen and wool. The patchwork was finished in 1928 and in 1930, a lovely print fabric was bought as a backing fabric. Sarah Monument lived in Stawell, Victoria, and died in 1952 after a long life.

Using small pieces of woollen fabrics, including lots of plaids and some felt, Alice Edith Farrer made a quilt in Warrnambool, Victoria. A woman who loved needlework of all kinds, she sewed, knitted and crocheted. Alice had only one child, a daughter, and the quilt was made for her in the early 1920s. (Her daughter recalled that in 1928 it was taken off her bed when the room was redecorated with pretty chintzes.) The quilt was sewn by machine,

and has a backing of lining fabric. Later, Alice was a loving and devoted grandmother to her daughter's four children, and also sewed for them. One of her grand-daughters fondly recalls an outfit that Alice made for her – a plaid skirt, with matching cap and bag. Alice died in 1965, aged eighty.

Even when only scraps of fabric were to hand, women used them to make something beautiful and to express their lives and ideas. Mary Jane Hannaford was one of Australia's most creative quiltmakers. Mary had come to Australia in 1842 when she was only two years old. Deserted just before her wedding day, she raised her only child, a daughter named Emily Agnes, who later married George Cady and had nine children. Mary primarily made quilts for her many grandchildren, and these quilts were meant to be used decoratively and hung. A family friend described Mary as a lovable lady, and she was long remembered in the Blandford district, New South Wales, for her church displays, especially those she did for Harvest Festival. Mary Hannaford continued to make quilts in her old age, as on her 'Time' quilt she embroidered her initials, 'M.J.H. Aged 84 years. 1924.' Mary died in 1930, aged ninety.

Several strong themes run through Mary's quilts – her religious faith, her love of Australia, and a melancholy sense of loss and time passing. She also loved nature, and her quilts are dotted with butterflies, insects, birds and animals. Mary's love of the country to which she had come was expressed in one quilt on the theme of 'Advance Australia Fair', and also in the many Australian birds and animals she used in her appliqué, although she did portray many others. In the quilt 'Adam and Eve in the Garden of Eden', Mary stitched an Eden full of birds, animals and trees, all worked with a joyous lack of perspective or relative size, so that a very Australian fly is bigger than a nearby hen with her chickens. A nativity is in the centre of the quilt, with the manger overlooked by four cows, and with an angel flying overhead. Underneath the nativity she worked the message, 'The Second Adam is Lord of Heaven and Earth'.

Mary used hand-appliqué to make her quilts. She cut scraps of fabric into shapes which she sewed onto large pieces of cotton as backgrounds. Details were added in the simplest of embroidery stitches. Mary's needle was her artist's tool, and although her techniques were simple and crude, she used them expressively with great conviction. Spaces on the quilts are filled with pieces of prints joined together to make strips which were then appliquéd in decorative patterns. Mary's descendants have a book of poems she copied out in 1861. Some of the same themes are found in this book as are seen on her quilts made some sixty years later — themes of death, loss and mother's love. The pages of the book are decorated with drawings of flowers and butterflies, the latter the same shapes as she appliquéd to her quilts.

On a quilt made in 1922, Mary appliquéd a wedding scene. A bride, with a long veil held by a little girl, is attended by two women, one holding a baby. The groom has an embroidered white beard and gold watch chain. An angel sprinkles the couple with embroidered flowers. Many birds are appliquéd to the quilt, including a swan, a dove and a large cockatoo with a crest of yellow stitching. There are also large leaves and berries, and a bunch of flowers tied with ribbon. Mary's characteristic pieced strips make the borders, with a final border of bright red around the outside. Two loops, handstitched at either side of the top of the quilt, indicate that the quilt was meant to be hung.

Mary Hannaford's 'Time' quilt has a large appliquéd clock with a poem on the theme of lost opportunities stitched beside it. Some of the lines say, ''Tis easy to squander our years/ In idleness folly and strife/ But oh! no repentance and tears/ Can bring back one moment of life'. There are flying angels as on many of her quilts, and in this quilt two angels flank Old Father Time. 'Farewell my dear ones Fare thee well' is worked under a portrait of an old lady in black carrying a cane and speaking to a couple. 'Goodbye' is nearby. It is fortunate that Mary Jane Hannaford's

wonderful quilts survived, as for a time they were put away in an old box out in a hay shed.

Many women at this time made Wagga rugs, although because of time and wear, not many remain in existence. Made as practical bedcovers, whatever was on hand was used in their construction, although usually an outer layer of cheap cretonne or simple patchwork hid the recycled fabrics of the inner layers. However, a small wagga made for a cot by Maude Thompson, of Narrandera, New South Wales, frankly shows the shapes of the knitted garments from which it was constructed. The knitted cardigans have been opened out and flattened, then decorated with spirals of wool embroidery, mainly in herringbone stitch. The little wagga is lined with plaid flannelette and the edge is finished with rows of crochet. It was made in the early 1920s for one of Maude's five daughters.

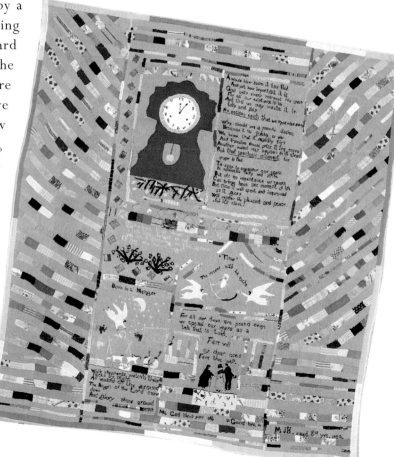

'TIME' QUILT MADE BY MARY JANE HANNAFORD. *154 cm x 164 cm (60 in x 64 in). Collection National Gallery of Australia, Canberra.*

WAGGA MADE BY MAUDE THOMPSON *(above).*
81 cm x 105 cm (32 in x 42 in). Private collection.
QUILT MADE BY CWA WOMEN *(right).*
298 cm x 288 cm (117 in x 110 in). Collection Euroa &
District Historical Society, Victoria.

Widowed when she was only thirty after her husband died of diphtheria, Maude lived very frugally. She was creative with her needle, and loved to use embroidery to decorate things in her home. She made her own embroidery patterns, and often used shapes taken from her garden.

The Country Women's Association, generally known by its initials as the CWA, was founded in Australia in 1922. Part of their motto is 'Service to the Country, Through Country Women, For Country Women, By Country Women'. They aimed to help rural women in very practical ways, such as by establishing rest rooms and baby health centres in country towns, improving maternity facilities in hospitals, teaching 'Domestic Science', and cutting down isolation by campaigning for an affordable telephone service. Another of their aims was 'To

encourage women and children to interest themselves in handicrafts and in beautifying their own homes and general surroundings'. Fund-raising was always an important activity, to have money to implement their aims. In the early 1930s, the women of the Euroa branch in Victoria made a quilt to raffle. The quilt was organised by Mrs Currie, the wife of Ian Currie who owned the large and prosperous Seven Creeks property. Mrs Currie had returned from England where she had seen beautiful needlework by the Royal School of Needlework, and was shown how to do patchwork. The quilt was made using an elongated hexagon as a pattern, and beautiful cotton print fabrics were cut precisely so as to centre motifs and match stripes. Every aspect of the quilt appears to have been carefully planned and executed. Some thirty women worked on the quilt, at first in their own homes and then at working bees which were frequently held at Mrs Currie's home. The quilt was exhibited at a State Home and Handicraft Exhibition in 1932, where it won a silver cup as the best piece of group work in the show. The raffle of the quilt raised sixty pounds, with tickets each sold for one shilling. To the dismay of the Euroa ladies, the quilt was won by a woman from New Zealand. However, Mrs Currie purchased the quilt back from the winner, so that it could stay in the Euroa district where the quilt remains to this day. Money from the raffle

BICA PHOTOGRAPHICS

was used variously to buy blankets for needy cases, for hospital expenses, and to support Somers House, a CWA holiday home at the beach.

The CWA women who sewed the lovely raffle quilt did not make only this prize-winning one. A CWA report notes that previously they had held working bees to make eighteen quilts out of 'waste material' to be sent to the Mallee, a district of Victoria hard-hit by dust, the rabbit plague and the Depression.

In country towns all around Australia, drapers and tailors had sample books of woollen suiting fabrics. Men ordering a suit to be made up could choose from these rectangles of fabric. Thrifty women took the outdated samples and made them into quilts which they generally called 'rugs'. The great number of these patchwork rugs existing today suggests that these must have been very common in country areas.

Caroline Bray, born in 1872, married Everett West, a grazier at Trundle, New South Wales. Sometime in the 1930s, Caroline used suiting samples she obtained from Tom Ellis the tailor to make patchwork rugs. In one rug, Caroline cut up the rectangular sample pieces into triangles, and alternated dark and light ones to make a strong pattern. She lined it with an old blanket, backed it with cotton twill and stitched the layers together at intervals with black lazy daisy stitches worked into a star shape. On a second rug which Caroline made, she mostly left the rectangular shapes as they were, the more usual way of making one of these rugs, but still she arranged the patches to balance the design and she alternated the light and darks to make a pattern.

Most newspapers at this time had a women's page which often featured needle-

RUG MADE BY CAROLINE WEST (top). 144 cm x 203 cm (57 in x 80 in). Collection Museum of Applied Arts and Sciences, Sydney.
'FARM LIFE QUILT' BY NETTIE HUPPATZ (left). 188 cm x 193 cm (74 in x 76 in). Collection Museum of Australia, Canberra.

work, crochet and knitting patterns. In March 1932 in South Australia, the *Adelaide Chronicle*, a weekly newspaper, began a new feature which was a competition to make a 'Farm Life Quilt'. Cash prizes were offered and the finished quilts were to be hung at the Royal Adelaide Show. There were two categories, one open and one for girls under eighteen. Published in weekly instalments through until June, the patterns showed animals — a horse, a dog, a rooster and a duck — as well as a tractor, a farmhouse and a barn. The barn makes it obvious that these were not Australian patterns, as Australian farms have sheds, not barns. The patterns were from Ruby Short McKim, an American quilt designer whose patterns were widely syndicated in the United States, and her name is in the corners of the designs.

The patterns appeared in a column under the name of 'Elizabeth George'. Women readers enjoyed what they called 'our' pages and wrote in letters. The hardship women were enduring from the Depression and Australia's uncertain climate is obvious in many letters. One wrote, 'A year ago my Digger husband lost home and everything owing to the drought, so since then I have had to keep my four children, and ourselves with what I can get for the cream from my three cows. It just keeps us in the bare necessities of food.' Another wrote that she found the Farm Life patterns an enjoyable change from regular sewing, as it was 'mend, mend, mend, mend these times, until there is little of the original article left'.

Twenty finished quilts were hung at the show and prizes were awarded. Minetta Huppatz, usually called Nettie, won first prize in the junior section with her quilt. Nettie lived on a farm at Eurelia, a tiny place some 250 kilometres from Adelaide. Like many children in remote areas, she had done her schooling by correspondence. The quilt shows great skill with the needle, no doubt taught by her

mother who won a prize in the open section. The shapes in the designs are filled in with rows of beautifully worked stem stitch. In the alternating squares of the quilt, each of which has been given its own separate square of wadding, Nettie quilted the horn of plenty design with back stitch, although the quilting does not go through to the back of the quilt. The quilt is interlined with an old blanket and lined with brown gingham.

In 1933 the *Adelaide Chronicle* began a new quilt series featuring Australian wildflowers. The response from readers was

KEN STEPNELL

'WILDFLOWER QUILT' BY NETTIE HUPPATZ *(above). 168 cm x 168 cm (66 in x 66 in). Collection Museum of Australia, Canberra.* NETTIE HUPPATZ *(right).*

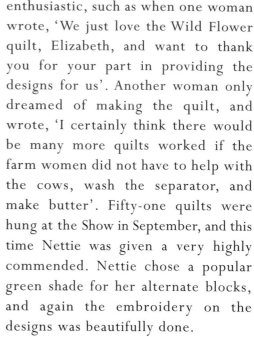

KEN STEPNELL

enthusiastic, such as when one woman wrote, 'We just love the Wild Flower quilt, Elizabeth, and want to thank you for your part in providing the designs for us'. Another woman only dreamed of making the quilt, and wrote, 'I certainly think there would be many more quilts worked if the farm women did not have to help with the cows, wash the separator, and make butter'. Fifty-one quilts were hung at the Show in September, and this time Nettie was given a very highly commended. Nettie chose a popular green shade for her alternate blocks, and again the embroidery on the designs was beautifully done.

The quilt competition was also syndicated to the Queensland paper, the *Queenslander*, in 1933. The patterns were published in the section of the paper titled 'Woman's Realm'. The quilts were hung at the Brisbane Exhibition of that year, with entries coming in from all over the state.

In 1934, the *Adelaide Chronicle* published patterns for an Australian bird quilt. Not only country women made these quilts, but also city women, such as Emily McKay who lived in an Adelaide suburb. Cream and green were her chosen colours for backgrounds.

It is not known who designed the Australian wildflower and bird quilts, although several of the wildflower designs are copied from drawings of Australian artist Eirene Mort. The *Adelaide Chronicle* continued publishing quilt patterns, but then returned to American designs. In 1937, they published one of the McKim quilt designs for children, the 'Three Little Pigs', and in 1938, they published the 'International quilt', with designs of places around the world. Nettie Huppatz also worked this quilt, embroidering each square with her customary skill.

Later, Nettie Huppatz married Laurie McColive, and she continued making quilts all her life. She especially loved to make quilts for children's charities as she was not blessed with the children of her own which she had hoped to have.

Isabella Cooke, the widow of Samuel Cooke, lived at Alstonville, in the Lismore area of New South Wales. Samuel Cooke had been a well-known breeder of dairy cattle in the area, and his sons were also involved in the work. Isabella made quilts for each of her six daughters and three sons. These quilts are rare for Australia, because they have an all-over pattern of quilting, but no patchwork or appliqué. Isabella's home, called 'Laurel Hill', had big wide verandahs, and Isabella used an enclosed one of these as a place to set up her quilting frame. This frame still exists within the family, and consists of two long pieces of kauri timber with webbing attached, and long iron bolts to act as stretchers at each end. The quilting frame was made by the local blacksmith in Alstonville. Isabella made her quilts from plain white cotton which she flat-quilted in a zigzag pattern with a thick

white cotton thread. Lines were ruled on the quilt to mark the pattern for stitching. The edges of the quilts are scalloped on three sides of the quilt and finished with a binding. A teacup was used to make the curved scallops. Isabella also made a quilt from show ribbons won by the family's cattle. The printing on the ribbons records wins at the Kyogle and Tweed River shows. The family were proud of their achievements in cattle breeding, and what better way of displaying it than through a quilt of blue ribbons? Isabella constructed the quilt by machine-stitching the ribbons onto a backing fabric of blue rayon brocade. She made a small bag of blue and gold ribbons in which to keep the quilt, and she also used ribbons to make jackets for her sons to wear. The dates on the ribbons are from the late 1920s and the 1930s. Isabella also exhibited her own needlework and cookery at agricultural shows. Isabella Cooke died in 1942, aged eighty-two.

QUILT OF SHOW RIBBONS MADE BY ISABELLA COOKE *(above). 141 cm x 183.3 cm (55 in x 72 in). Collection of the National Gallery of Australia, Canberra.*
QUILT MADE BY ISABELLA COOKE *(left). 212 cm x 276 cm (84 in x 109 in). Collection National Gallery of Australia, Canberra.*
QUILT MADE BY EMILY MCKAY *(top left). 165 cm x 204 cm (65 in x 80 in). Private collection.*

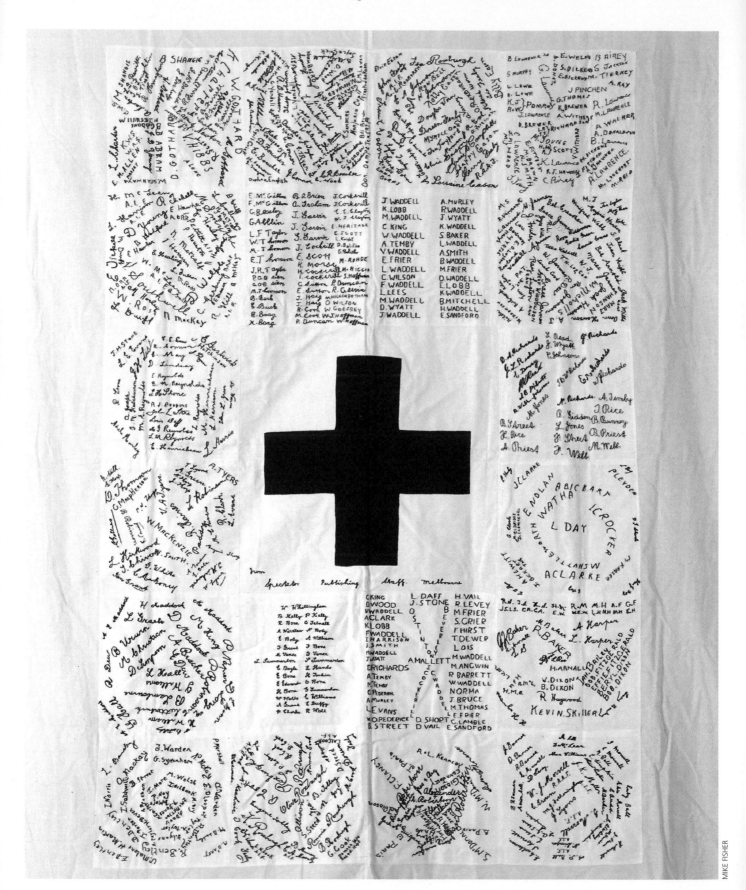

QUILT MADE BY STAFF OF THE SPECTATOR PUBLISHING COMPANY.

184 cm x 223 cm (72 in x 88 in). Collection Australian Red Cross Society, Victorian Division.

1939 TO 1945

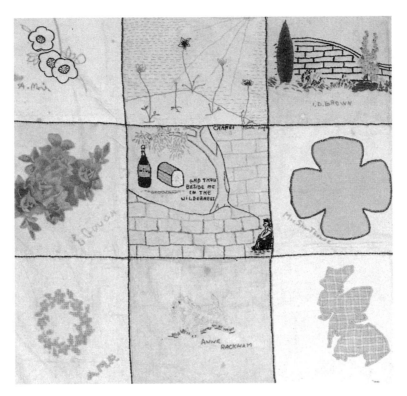

DETAIL OF QUILT MADE FOR THE AUSTRALIAN SOLDIERS.

On 3 September 1939, it was the 'melancholy duty' of Prime Minister Robert Menzies to tell Australians that they were once again at war. In Europe, Hitler's Germany had attacked Poland, precipitating Britain and her allies to fight. Australia, as part of the British Commonwealth, also declared war against Germany. In December 1941, Australia had a new and closer enemy when Japan simultaneously attacked the Americans in Hawaii and the British in Malaya. Australian troops fought in Europe and North Africa, but with the Japanese attacking throughout the Pacific area, Australian troops were needed nearer to home, to defend the Malay Peninsula and Singapore, and even Australia itself.

Unlike the First World War, more roles opened up for women during the Second World War. With men away at the war, women went into factory jobs and joined the Women's Land Army. There were nursing and medical jobs through the Australian Army Nursing Service (AANS) and the Australian Army Medical Women's Service (AAMWS). Women enlisted through the Australian Women's Army Service (AWAS), the Women's Australian Auxiliary Airforce (WAAF) and the Women's Royal Australian Naval Service (WRANS).

The need for Red Cross work continued, and once again signature quilts were made to raise money. One quilt was made by the staff of the Spectator Publishing Company in Melbourne, a printing company whose prime responsibility was to publish the weekly Methodist paper, the *Spectator*. The quilt has a large red cross appliquéd in the centre, surrounded by blocks filled with signatures embroidered in red. The manager of the company was J.E. Poppins, the author's grandfather. His name is not on the quilt, but there are names belonging to his wife's family, the Stones, including Louisa Stone, his sister-in-law, who worked as a clerk in the company. His daughter's name, A.J. Poppins, is there, as well as many other members of his church, the Fairfield Methodist Church. In fact, many of the family names on the church's 1939–45 Honour Roll are found on the quilt. The name Waddell appears many times on the quilt, as Will Waddell worked for the *Spectator* and the Waddells were members of the Fairfield church.

General Sir Thomas Blamey, originally from Wagga Wagga, New South Wales, was made the commander of the Allied land forces in the

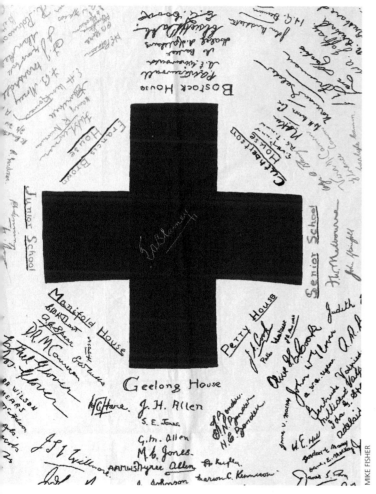

Southwestern Pacific from 1942 to 1945. During the summer of 1942/43, he was in command of the fighting against the Japanese in New Guinea. General Blamey's signature is embroidered in the centre of a Red Cross quilt worked by Mrs Gladys Mountford, with assistance from students of the Geelong Grammar School, a wealthy private school in Victoria. Mrs Mountford was the wife of the school chaplain, and the signatures are grouped under the house names of the school. Many of the

names were of old boys who had enlisted. The quilt was worked on from 1940 through to 1945.

Another Red Cross quilt is completely different. It is totally made from detachable shirt collars which have been neatly stitched together by machine. The collars are stitched into rows, with more collars making an outside border. The button-holes, where studs would join the collar to the neck of the shirt, can be seen. The quilt is backed with cotton and machine-quilted. Inked on a back corner of the quilt is the inscription, 'Made by Mrs C A Hewett 30.8.40 Wokurna P.O. S.A.', and near it there is a stamp saying 'Australian Red Cross Society South Australia'. The present owner of the quilt tried to find out more about the maker, and managed to track down Mrs Hewett's daughter.

The Hewett family lived on a mixed farm at Wokurna, South Australia. There were three children, the daughter and two older boys. According to her daughter, Caroline Hewett was a very accomplished needlewoman, both in hand-sewing and machine-sewing on her Singer treadle machine. She made 'practically everything' the family used, including soap, jam, preserves and pickled meat — and all this without modern conveniences, such as a washing machine, fridge or running water in the house. She sewed all of her own and her daughter's clothes, usually making the latter from material from her own old frocks. Caroline made more than one shirt collar quilt as her daughter remembers her working on them, along with a group of local ladies who worked for the Red Cross during the war years. Besides sewing, they knitted socks and bala-clavas, and baked cakes which were put into tins and sent overseas. Caroline died in 1960, aged seventy.

Shortages and rationing in Australia meant that new fabric was scarce, so scraps, samples and used clothing were conserved and used to make quilts and Wagga rugs, among other things. In 1942, Delia Williamson made a wagga with samples of fabric that was called 'physician flannel', a striped wool and cotton fabric which was extensively used to make winter pyjamas. The wagga was filled with used clothing, and the layers stitched together by machine. Delia, not yet married at this time, lived with her family in Kandos, New South Wales, where her father was a dentist. The family had many waggas which by day were folded at the end of the bed on top of a bedspread. Darker waggas were used for camping. The family pet name for a wagga was 'woggle'.

Singapore was believed to be the 'impregnable fortress', so it was a major defeat for the Allies when the Japanese successfully fought their way down the Malay peninsula and forced Singapore to surrender in February 1942. The Japanese took seventy thousand soldiers prisoner, including fifteen thousand Australians. A group of women and children were swept up in the maelstrom of the final chaotic days in Singapore. The group numbered about five hundred people, including some military wives, some families of planters and European administrators, and also civilian nurses, doctors, teachers, missionaries and a few older women who had been left behind. Mostly the women were European, although there were some Eurasians.

The military prisoners of war, the POWs, were herded into vast camps in the Changi area of Singapore Island. The civilian internees, both men and women, were put into Changi gaol. This gaol had been recently built to hold six hundred Asiatic prisoners, but two thousand eight hundred internees were crowded into it. The men and women were strictly segregated, and punishment was swift for those who broke the rules.

Boredom was one of the problems of imprisonment, so activities were begun to overcome it. Elizabeth Ennis, a nurse, began a Girl Guide group, and she was assisted by a young Dutch woman, Trudie van Roode. Trudie had the idea of getting the girls to make a quilt, so they sewed hexagon

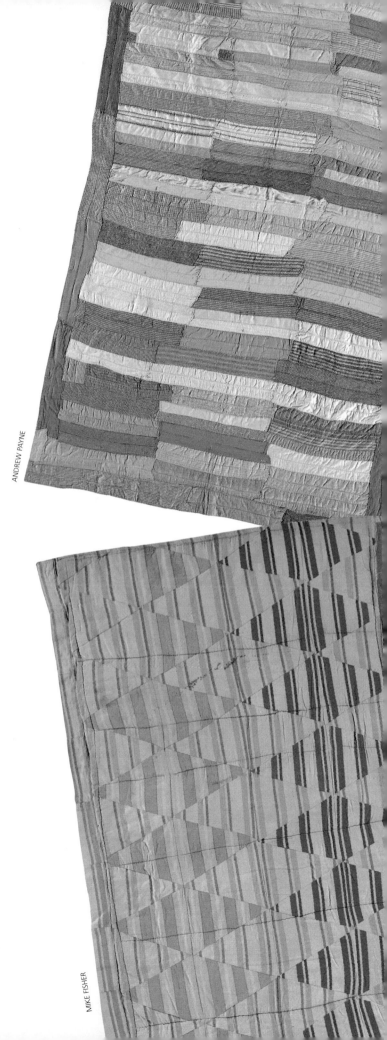

QUILT MADE BY CAROLINE HEWETT *(top). 126 cm x 218 cm (50 in x 86 in). Private collection.*
WAGGA MADE BY DELIA WILLIAMSON *(right). 98 cm x 157 cm (38 in x 62 in). Collection Pioneer Women's Hut, Tumbarumba, New South Wales.*
DETAIL OF QUILT SHOWING BLAMEY SIGNATURE *(left). Collection Australian Red Cross Society, Victorian Division.*

patches together into rosettes and put their names or initials in the centres. Ethel Mulvaney, a Canadian who was the unofficial Red Cross leader in the women's camp, saw the patchwork and suggested the women could make quilts for the Red Cross. The idea was that the quilts could be a vehicle of communication to the men in the big military camps nearby. At first only wives of the military were to be involved, but then the project was broadened to the other women. Squares of white fabric were given out, and each woman was asked to 'put something of themselves' as well as their name into the square. Some of the women made several squares. The quality of the embroidery varied, with some showing very skilled hands while others stitched more crudely. The squares were joined together to make three quilts, each with sixty-six squares. A message was stitched onto the back of each quilt. One·inscription read, 'Presented by the women of Changi Internment Camp 1942 to the wounded Australian soldiers with our sympathy for their suffering. It is our wish that on cessation of hostilities that this quilt be presented to the Australian Red Cross Society. It is advisable to dry clean this quilt.' The other two quilts had the same message, except that one named the 'British soldiers' and the 'British Red Cross', and the other named the 'Nipponese soldiers' and the 'Japanese Red Cross'.

The women hoped that by being even-handed in their sympathy, the quilts would be allowed to reach their intended destination, the hospital in the big Changi military POW camp. Once there, the quilts would be a reassuring communication of names and messages to the men. This intention succeeded, because the quilts were sent to the men's camp.

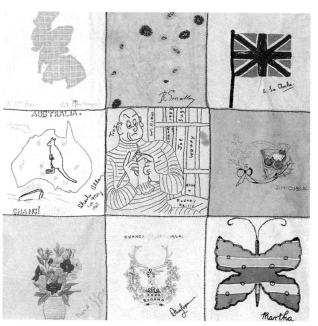

DETAIL OF QUILT MADE FOR THE AUSTRALIAN SOLDIERS.

Captain J. Ennis, a British military doctor, who had married Elizabeth just days before the surrender, saw the quilts after their arrival at the camp.

The quilt intended for the Japanese soldiers is different from the other two quilts. In the top left corner is a greeting in Japanese, and most of the motifs on the quilt are pretty flowers. Other motifs include the sun rising over the water and an oriental bridge, so it would seem the women wanted to use images that might please the Japanese.

The real message was always there, though, through the embroidered names. Freddy Bloom added more than just a flower and her name to her square. Next to her daffodil she embroidered the words 'Daffodil rampant', presumably a message for her doctor husband, Philip, whom she had married just days before Singapore fell and who was in the Changi POW camp.

The quilt made for the Australian soldiers and the quilt made for the British soldiers have other motifs besides a few squares with flowers on them. The women embroidered patriotic images, such as the British flag, 'V' for victory signs, St George slaying the dragon, and Drake at his bowls. There are messages of optimism, such as 'Hope Springs Eternal in the Human Breast' and a grinning soldier with his thumbs up. Some of the messages are humorous, such as 'A room with a view' showing the prison cell with underwear hanging in the barred window, and another which announces that 'There will always an England as long as Scotland stands'. Freddy Bloom embroidered a clock with wings, a reflection of her determination to be positive about making time fly. One square shows a brick wall with the ironic words 'Changi holiday home'. The grim environment is

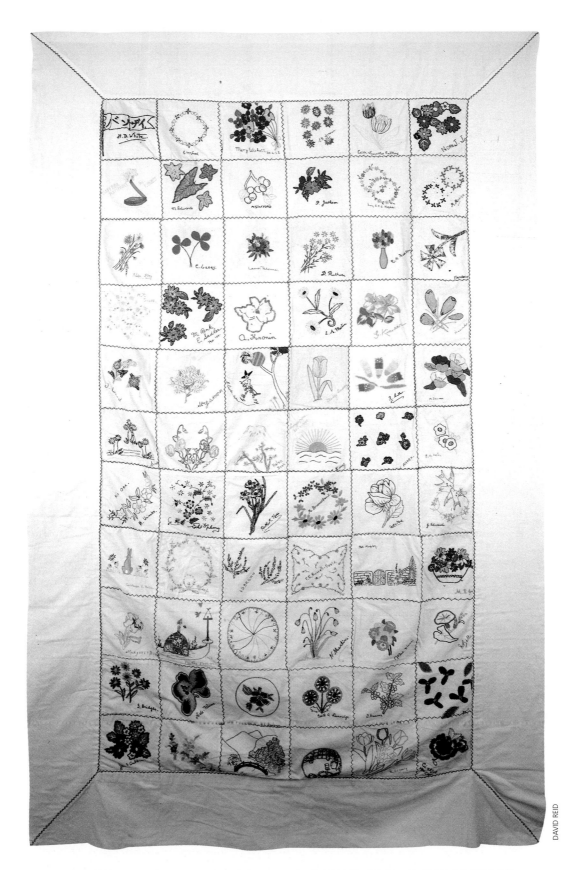

DAVID REID

QUILT MADE BY CIVILIAN INTERNEES IN CHANGI GAOL, WITH MESSAGE FOR THE NIPPONESE SOLDIERS. *134 cm x 165 cm (53 in x 65 in). Collection Australian War Memorial, Canberra.*

portrayed in Lady Katherine Heath's square which shows the prison tower through a barred window. The recent experiences of some of the internees is revealed in one square with a map of the Malay peninsula, and arrows which mark the retreat down to Singapore. Elizabeth Ennis embroidered a large boat and 'Homeward Bound', a reference to the honeymoon she had hoped to have on the journey back to England. Some squares have private messages, such as the birth of a baby boy shown by an embroidered blue ribbon. Most poignant of all is the square which shows a tiny figure huddled in the corner of a cell with the words 'How long O Lord How long!'

Sheila Allan was just seventeen years old, a young girl who had only just finished her convent education. Her father, John Charles Allan, had been an Australian mining engineer working in Malaya, and her mother, whom Sheila had barely known was a Malay. Sheila, her father and her Malay stepmother, had escaped down the Malay peninsula to Singapore just ahead of the advancing Japanese army. Dreaming of Australia, her father's homeland which she had never visited, Sheila embroidered a map of Australia with a kangaroo in the centre on her block. Underneath the map she embroidered 'Changi', and the word 'Prison' can just be detected next to it, although it was not embroidered.

The quilts were made in the early months of internment, a time when the women hoped that soon they would be repatriated home. It was also a time when some of them had more in the way of fabric and threads which they had brought with them into internment. Little did they then know that they would have to endure the overcrowding,

an increasingly inadequate diet, and the oppressive confinement, until the end of the war in August 1945. In May 1944, the women were moved to a camp in Sime Road, and military POWs were moved into Changi gaol.

Most of the women survived the internment, although a few of them suffered more than the rest. In October 1943, the Japanese secret police suspected Freddy Bloom of spying, even though she explained that one of the things they thought suspicious was just some braille she was learning as a camp activity, and that all it said was 'Mary had a little lamb'. Freddy was taken out of Changi and put into another gaol for five months. She shared a grim cell with a group of men who were brutally treated by the guards. Fortunately, Freddy was not tortured, but she eventually collapsed from beriberi, and was returned to Changi gaol. After the war, Freddy was reunited with Philip and they settled in London.

Sheila Allan's father died during internment and was buried in Singapore. After the war, Sheila went to live with her father's sister in Australia, and she trained to become a nurse. Both Sheila and Freddy kept diaries during internment, and these have been published in recent years.

At the end of the war, two of the Changi quilts were sent to the Australian and British Red Cross as requested in the messages on their backs. The Japanese were not interested in the quilt destined for their Red Cross, so an Australian, Lt Col R.M.W. Webster, took the quilt back to his wife. Later, Mrs Webster donated the quilt to the Australian War Memorial in Canberra where it was eventually joined by the Australian quilt.

DAVID REID

QUILT MADE BY CIVILIAN INTERNEES IN CHANGI GAOL, WITH MESSAGE FOR THE AUSTRALIAN SOLDIERS *(above)*. *130 cm x 203 cm (51 in x 80 in). Collection Australian War Memorial, Canberra.*
SHEILA ALLAN *(left)*.

DETAIL OF QUILT MADE BY GLADYS WILLIAMS.
Private collection.

ANDREW SIKORSKI

1946 TO 1969

QUILT MADE BY HILDA KLUUKERI *(above)*.
150 cm x 188 cm (59 in x 74 in). Private collection.

After the Second World War, Australia entered a long period of growth and prosperity, although there were interruptions, such as the Korean War and the Vietnam War, and the Cold War loomed in the background. The population expanded as migrants from Britain and Europe were encouraged to settle in sunny Australia, and the society gradually became more cosmopolitan and less insular. However, Australia still remained intensely loyal to Britain, and turned out with great enthusiasm when the young Queen Elizabeth visited in 1954. Suburbs steadily sprawled outward from the city centres with most families living in their own detached homes. Ordinary people now had cars, and women began to take conveniences like washing machines and refrigerators for granted. In 1966, Australia began the long process of becoming a metric country.

In spite of the changes in women's jobs brought about by the war, most women still saw their main role as being at home with the family. But with growing prosperity, remnants and reminders of the hard times, the 'make do and mend', were discarded. The fashion was for cotton chenille and other bought bedspreads, and the making of patchwork quilts generally, although not completely, declined. It was a lean time for quiltmaking in Australia.

Hexagon patchwork remained a perennial favourite. In 1957, Mrs Gladys Williams, of Albury, New South Wales, finished a quilt which she had begun in the late 1930s. The quilt was begun when Gladys was staying with her sister, a dressmaker, in Tasmania. She was helping to tidy up, and asked what she could do with the leftover scraps of fabric. 'Burn them,' replied her sister. Unwilling to

81

ANDREW SIKORSKI

pool. A young Ron Clarke was the Australian chosen to carry the torch into the stadium to light the Olympic flame. A little bit of Olympic fever is captured in a simple quilt made by Hilda Loviisa Kluukeri, in Tully, Queensland, in 1957 or 1958. The quilt was made for her oldest grand-daughter, Bev Frazer, because she loved the quilt that Hilda had made for Bev's mother. Hilda collected dress-making scraps from her daughter's sewing and also from a neighbour who was a dressmaker. The grand-daughter can still recall where most of the fabrics came from — her own dresses, a baby sister's rompers, her mother's dresses and a dressing gown, her father's pyjamas, and her brother's shirts. The Olympic fabric was from a shirt made for Bev's brother who started school in 1957. The print shows the Olympic rings and figures running with the Olympic torch. The quilt was sewn on a treadle sewing machine, and consists of large triangles. It is lined with an old piece of chenille and is backed with a grey cotton print which has been brought to the front as an edge finish. Hilda originally came from Finland, migrating to Australia in 1923 with her husband Johannes. They settled on cane farms, first near Ingham, then in Tully. Hilda lived by an old Finnish proverb which translates to the English 'waste not, want not'. Her grand-daughter, Bev, cherishes her special quilt, and when her children were young, they liked to 'read the quilt' and listen to stories of the people from whose garments the pieces came.

A few crazy quilts continued to be made in the 1950s. Jean Joyce made a quilt because she too had to spend hours by a sick bed, in her case with an invalid husband. Not wanting to 'just sit there' and because she loved to sew, Jean began the quilt with leftover cotton dressmaking scraps which were given to her by a friend. She left the patches in the odd shapes as they were given, and arranged them onto unbleached calico which she had joined together

do this, Gladys decided to take them home to make a patchwork cushion, and this eventually grew into a quilt. Not one to ever sit with idle hands, Gladys was glad to have the patchwork to do when sitting at the bedside of her children when they were ill, and, as one of her two boys suffered very badly from asthma, she had to sit up quite frequently. The patchwork was kept in a big biscuit tin so that she could take it with her to sew. Gladys stayed with her family in Tasmania during the war years when her husband was overseas fighting in North Africa. The family returned to their home in Albury after the war, where another son was born. Gladys used scraps from family dresses in the quilt, and can recall which fabrics came from her mother, mother-in-law and a friend. When assembling the quilt, she laid out the rosettes of hexagons on a bed and spent some time arranging them so as to gain the best effect. A woman who sewed beautifully, Gladys recalls her mother's maxim, 'If a job is worth doing, it is worth doing well'. The quilt is backed with a lovely heavy pale blue moire which was bought specially, although it was a bargain at the time because it was slightly faded.

In 1956 the Olympic Games were held in Melbourne. Australia has always been a sport-loving nation and there was great enthusiasm for the Games. To the delight of the nation, Australians won thirteen gold medals and dominated the swimming

DETAIL OF OLYMPIC PRINT (top).
QUILT MADE BY JEAN JOYCE (right). 177 cm x 215 cm (70 in x 85 in). Collection Pioneer Women's Hut, Tumbarumba, New South Wales.

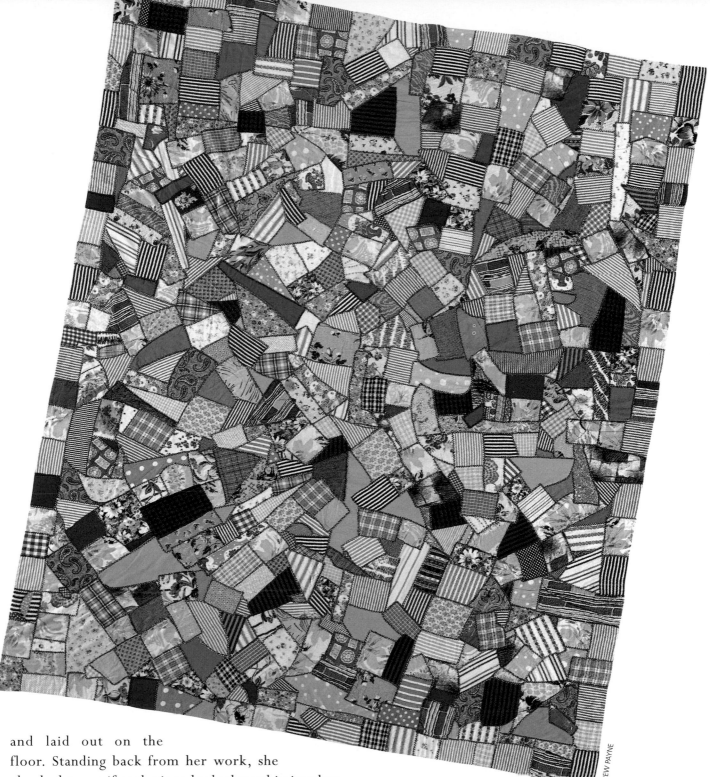

and laid out on the floor. Standing back from her work, she checked to see if each piece looked good in its place, then pinned it down. The pieces were sewn to the calico with red thread using a neat and even herringbone stitch. The finished quilt was given to her sister, Joan Bolton, as a Christmas present. Jean made two other quilts in the same manner, and Joan used them in her holiday house at the coast. Later, Jean made many quilts in the technique which she calls 'Boston Daisy', using a method of making the patches the same as Suffolk Puffs, only the gathered circles are joined in groups of seven to make flower-like rosettes.

By the end of the sixties very few women were making quilts. Those that were mostly made hexagon quilts, so much so that, to many Australians, patchwork meant hexagons. The pieced-over-papers English style was taught through the embroiderer's guilds which were established in the late 1950s and 1960s, and this also helped keep the style alive.

QUILT MADE BY MARJORIE COLEMAN (above), 'Dullflower No 2: Macrocarpa ... Rose of the West', 1984.
173 cm x 238 cm (68 in x 94 in). Collection of National Gallery of Australia, Canberra.
QUILT MADE BY BARBARA MACEY (right), 'Metamorphosis of an Undergound Landscape', 1986. 170 cm x 230 cm (67 in x 91 in).

1970 TO THE PRESENT . . .

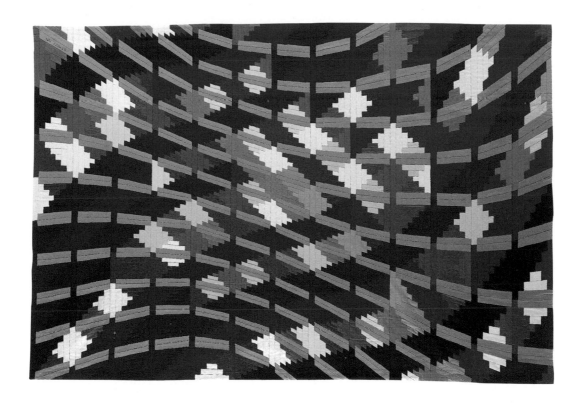

From 1970 onwards, Australia increasingly became part of the international world. Television, now in almost every home, beamed a wider world into living rooms. Airline travel meant people worked and holidayed abroad with great ease. More young people went into higher education, and many studied overseas. Women's roles changed radically as most began to combine work outside the home with their domestic responsibilities. Australia became more independent from Britain as political, legal and trading ties diminished or disappeared. American culture, through films, television, fast-food chains and clothing, became more influential. Trade increased with nearby Asian nations. Many people enjoyed a higher standard of living than ever before, with comfortable suburban houses, cars, and electrical appliances for all possible purposes, although persistent unemployment meant not all of society participated in this affluence.

Quiltmaking was influenced by these trends towards internationalisation. In the United States, quiltmaking, always a strong traditional craft, was undergoing a major revival. Three factors particularly influenced this revival. In 1971 there was an exhibition of quilts, titled Abstract Design in American Quilts, at the Whitney Museum of American Art in New York. The hitherto humble quilt was recognised as art. Another factor was the Bicentennial celebrations in 1976, when American women looked affectionately and patriotically to their past, and this revealed the marvellous richness of quilts which were in such abundance around them. Also important was the women's movement, which created an atmosphere in which women wanted their achievements recognised, and the newly discovered heritage of quilts obviously had predominantly been created by women. Not that most women who enthusiastically took up quilting saw themselves as feminists, but the mind-set of desiring recognition for women was important.

Australian women who lived in the United States in the 1970s and 1980s were exposed to the American tradition and became caught up in the enthusiasm of the time and the possibilities that the craft of quilting offered. They brought back to Australia new ideas about making quilts, with the emphasis on a different style of piecing, American block designs and decorative quilting. Marjorie Coleman, from Perth, was inspired by Hawaiian quilts in the early seventies. Trudy Billingsley, from Sydney, lived in Toronto, Canada, in the early seventies and began making quilts there. The author, from Canberra, visited Los Angeles in 1975, just before the American Bicentennial. Noni Fisher, from Sydney, lived in Houston, Texas in the late seventies. Trudi Brodie and Narelle Grieve, both also from Sydney, lived in the United States for a time during the late seventies and early eighties. These women returned to Australia enthusiastic about the craft which they had either seen or learned about. There were others as well, but these were some of the Australians who continued to make quilts, and most of them went on to teach quiltmaking and become active in the formation of quilting groups.

Not that the influence from the United States was the whole story. The craft of quiltmaking fell on fertile ground in Australia because of the general interest in craft which had gathered momentum from the 1960s and had grown into an organised movement in the 1970s with the establishment of state and territory crafts councils. Interest in embroidery was increasing, and embroiderers' guilds were already well-established around the country.

Then there were individuals like Barbara Macey, of Melbourne, who became interested in quiltmaking from realising the possibilities inherent in a Log Cabin block which she happened to see in an embroidery book. Intensely interested in perception from her university studies in psychology, she explored the potential for illusion through the medium of Log Cabin patchwork. Working on her own, she was able to manipulate the Log Cabin block to make curves from straight lines. Barbara put together combinations of bright strong colours, or played on the subtleties of black and deep dark colours. By the mid-1980s she was exhibiting in fibre and craft shows, and in 1985 her 'Red Quilt', made in 1983, was accepted for Quilt National, the major American contemporary quilt exhibition. Barbara sewed her Log Cabin blocks onto a prepared foundation fabric, and the quilts were then backed and bound around the edges, with little or no quilting added. Later, Barbara created quilts using crazy patchwork, and these were also made by sewing onto a foundation fabric.

Another unique individual was Dora Grose, from Broken Hill, with her lifelong interest in patchwork. Originally Dora Sergeant, she first made Wagga rugs from suiting samples when only a teenager in the late 1920s and early 1930s. Dora begged the samples from the tailor for whom her widowed mother worked. She sewed the samples together, backed them with wheat or bran bags, and added embroidery around the edges of the patches. Later, she began her first quilt using a shape she called a 'Church window', using the English method of piecing over papers. Her husband, Alf Grose, cut out the original template. However, she did not complete the quilt for many years as she was busy with a growing family. Seeing a quilt called a 'Martha Washington Rose' in an Australian magazine in 1962, she corresponded with the maker, a Canadian woman living in Australia. The pattern she so admired is usually called a 'Grandmother's Flower Garden', with hexagons sewn around a centre to make a rosette. This pattern became Dora's favourite. She liked to use 'Rose' in the names she gave to her quilts, such as a quilt she made for the Silverlea children's charity which she called 'Silverlea Rose', and a quilt she named 'Charlotte's Roses' after her grandmother and great-grandmother, both of whom were called Charlotte. In the early 1980s, Dora ran classes teaching other people how to make quilts, especially the hexagon quilts. As the new techniques from America became widespread, Dora added these to her repertoire, and made many more quilts. But throughout the rest of her life she continued to make hexagon quilts using the English method. Her quilts were given away to charities or to her family; altogether, Dora Grose made more than thirty quilts. She died in March 1993.

When Australians first began to take up American-style quilting in the 1970s, there were very few books available and no special quilting fabrics or threads. Supplies were gleaned from dressmaking fabric shops, and winter was an especially lean time when cotton fabrics were withdrawn for the season. Quilting hoops and quilting threads had either to be specially imported or replaced with substitutes. In the early 1980s, quilting shops began to be opened. Often these began from a home, then expanded into shop premises, such as Margaret Williams' Patchwork House in Melbourne and Ruth Stoneley's Patchwork Supplies in Brisbane. Shops opened in all parts of Australia. In Sydney, American Jean Drury had a shop for some time, Diana Challinor began the Quilting Bee, and Val Moore started a shop in Pennant Hills. In Perth, Lois McCarthy opened Patchworks of WA. At first, these shop pioneers had to import directly from the United States as the local importing businesses lacked interest. As more and more shops opened, a 'quilting industry' was established in Australia, with importers and wholesalers becoming involved as they realised the potential strength of interest in quilting.

Unlike quiltmakers from Australia prior to the 1970s, where quiltmaking was always the work of the individual sewing alone, the new generation of women taking up quilting wanted to get together to learn, to make, and to share their new-found interest. Quilting groups sprang up all over Australia; the first was in Canberra, where a small advertisement in the *Canberra Times* on 12 June 1976 invited interested people to get together, thus sowing the seed which grew to be Canberra Quilters. Only a little later that year, a group of women in Western Australia met on 23 August, and the Western Australian Quilters' Association was born. In 1978, the Patchworkers and Quilters Guild formed in

Victoria, and in 1979, Megan Terry became the inaugural president of the Quilter's Association of Victoria, which later became the Australian Quilter's Association. Other states followed, with the Quilters' Guild of New South Wales beginning in 1982, and the Tasmanian Guild, the Queensland Quilters and the Darwin Patchworkers and Quilters all began in 1983. In 1984, the Quilters' Guild of South Australia was started. Victorian Quilters was established in 1993. As the major state groups grew, they became more formalised. Hundreds of women around Australia loyally served on committees, published newsletters, ran meetings, operated libraries of quilt books, set up teaching workshops, and organised annual or biennial exhibitions of their quilts. In the early 1990s, the state and territory groups sent delegates to form the Australian Council of Quilters. Since then, this group has met annually in different states.

DORA GROSE

ANDREW SIKORSKI

QUILT DESIGN BY MARGARET ROLFE *(above), 'Penguin Parade'. Sewn by Beth Miller, 1989. 118 cm x 144 cm (46 in x 57 in). Private collection.*
QUILT MADE BY JAN IRVINE *(right). 'Aerodrome', 1988. 120 cm x 250 cm (48 in x 100 in). Collection of Museum of Applied Arts and Sciences, Sydney.*

small and large, created a strong network for women, celebrating birthdays and special events, such as the birth of children and grandchildren, and offering sympathetic support through illness and death.

Women with quilting skills soon found themselves being asked to teach. Many taught from home, but as shops and quilting groups developed, these offered teaching opportunities. Some quilters became professional quilt teachers and travelled extensively throughout Australia. Most of the state and territory groups established Teacher Accreditation programmes in order to foster high standards of teaching and craftsmanship, and also to assist people in learning how to become a teacher. This formalised teaching was in complete contrast to the individual learning in the domestic environment which happened in the past, but was consistent with more and more activities being sourced from outside the home.

The large state groups were not the only ones to form. Independent groups were created in suburban regions and country towns. Hosts of quilters joined 'friendship groups', small groups of women who met regularly in each other's homes to quilt and to chat. All these groups,

Books were written, beginning with the author's *Australian Patchwork* and Deborah Brearley's *Patches of Australia* in 1985. Both books feature original Australian patterns for pieced wildflowers and appliquéd birds and animals. Numerous other books on quilting have followed, including Susan Denton and Barbara Macey's *Quiltmaking* and Dianne Finnegan's *Piece by Piece* and *Quilters' Kaleidoscope*, books which particularly feature the work of Australian quiltmakers. Magazines also began, with *Down Under Quilts* beginning in 1988, and *Australian Patchwork and Quilting* following in 1994.

While many Australians who were interested in quilting first made mostly traditional-style American quilts, and thus learned the American techniques, many went on to use their newly learned skills to make their own original quilts, often with Australian themes. For example, Marjorie Coleman made a quilt inspired by the unique and beautiful blooms of the Western Australian macrocarpa tree. The title she gave to the quilt is an ironic barb at the past disdain for Australian wildflowers, 'Dullflower ... No. 2: Macrocarpa ... Rose of the West'. The wildflower

design was made by hand-appliqué, and the quilt was intricately hand-quilted. The author, Margaret Rolfe, created pieced block designs of Australian animals. Her quilt design 'Penguin Parade' captured fairy penguins waddling up the beach, a unique sight seen on some of Australia's southern coastline.

In 1988, the celebration of the Bicentennial of European settlement in Australia gave a great impetus to quiltmaking. Australian subjects, especially of the landscape and the flora and fauna, were especially popular. The Quilters' Guild held a major exhibition called Quilt Australia '88, at Centrepoint, in the heart of Sydney, in June 1988. Jan Irvine's quilt 'Aerodrome' was a brilliant and sophisticated response to the Bicentennial theme. Originally trained as an art teacher, Jan Irvine is one of the many women who came to quilting from an interest in textiles. The family influence was strong, as Jan inherited rag rugs from her great-grandmother, crochet from her grandmother, and

ANDREW SIKORSKI

making came from America, with designs produced for the big American market. Some Australian fabrics with Australian motifs were produced, particularly in the 1990s, and many of these featured Australian flora and Aboriginal designs.

Although Australia was by now a country which generally used metric measurements, quilters were reluctant to change from imperial measurements, and this reluctance was reinforced by the extensive importation of American books, magazines, and quiltmaking tools.

Whether displayed in small or large exhibitions, or brought out at meetings for 'Show and tell', most of the quilts made during the 1980s and 1990s were for a quilter's family use or for her own home. A quick glance at most quilt exhibition catalogues shows quilts

embroidery from her mother. Jan turned to airbrushing her images onto fabric when she became frustrated with the definition of edge in her work. Jan uses close hand-quilting to give gentle relief and texture to her pieces. Her image for the Bicentennial captures Australia's wide brown land and spectacular starry skies, with modern European man represented by the windsock flag and the Aboriginal people alluded to both in the glimpse of the Aboriginal flag inside the windsock and in the pattern of earth forms below it.

Australian women relied heavily on imported fabrics for their quiltmaking, in the same way as Australians have always done for most textiles because Australia has never been a textile-producing country. Most fabrics imported for quilt-

QUILT MADE BY TRICIA BOWDLER (top),
'Ninety Not Out', 1997. 170 cm x 186 cm (67 in x 73 in).
QUILT MADE BY KATIE FRIEND (right),
'Kelburn', 1997. 144 cm x 218 cm (57 in x 86 in).
QUILT MADE BY KERRY GAVIN (far right),
'Where Eagles Dare', 1997. 211 cm x 211 cm (83 in x 83 in).

ANDREW PAYNE

ANDREW PAYNE

made for children and grandchildren, nieces and nephews, parents, friends, husbands and wedding anniversaries. In the 1997 Canberra Quilters Exhibition, Tricia Bowdler showed a quilt which she had made for her mother's ninetieth birthday. Tricia called the quilt 'Ninety not out', an obvious reference to her mother's special birthday, but also an allusion to her mother's lifelong love of cricket. A simple scrap quilt, Tricia's quilt has ninety hearts

machine-appliquéd on it and it is machine-quilted.

Quilters also made quilts for other reasons – to remember places where they had lived or visited, to explore new designs, or to enjoy using fabrics and techniques they particularly liked. Quilts were made in all sizes, from small and miniature quilts, through to large king-size quilts. The smaller quilts, whether traditional or innovative in design, were made to hang on walls rather than to be used on

ANDREW SIKORSKI

Australians learned the American vocabulary for quilting, such as 'block', 'batting', 'piecing', and 'print' (used to describe fabric) and they became familiar with American block names, such as the Ohio Star, Clay's Choice, and Sunbonnet Sue. From being an almost unknown skill, hand-quilting became widespread. In the 1990s, machine-quilting increased and became acceptable in its own right. Australian quilters learned the new skills of American quilting well, and a few exhibited quilts in major quilt shows in the United States. The American Quilters' Society's annual show, held at Paducah, Kentucky, sets very high standards of workmanship in piecing, quilting and appliqué, and only selected quilts are hung. A number of Australian quilters have had work chosen, and some have won awards. In 1992, Kerry

QUILT MADE BY CANBERRA QUILTERS *(above),*
Barbara Goddard, Beryl Hodges, Kerry Gavin, Judy Turner
and the author, 1997. 213 cm x 213 cm (84in x 84 in).
QUILT MADE BY JUDY HOOWORTH *(right),*
'Composition in Yellow', 1993. 205 cm x 210 cm (81 in x 83 in).

beds. Katie Friend made a special quilt to celebrate her own place, a country property called 'Kelburn' in the Goulburn area of New South Wales. The quilt shows a two-storey stone house which was built on the property in 1831. There is also the homestead and stables, built from brick in 1899, and a large windmill, a characteristic structure found throughout country Australia. Sheep, which the district is famous for, wander into the quilt's borders. The quilt was pieced by both machine and hand, and was appliquéd and quilted by hand.

Gavin, of Canberra, won an Honourable Mention for her pieced, hand-quilted and trapuntoed quilt 'Flight of Forty', and a year later, won a third prize for her appliquéd, hand-quilted and trapuntoed quilt, 'On Wings of Freedom'. Kerry's immaculate piecing, and her skill and dedication with the quilting needle, became well known throughout Australia, and is shown in her quilt 'Where Eagles Dare', finished in 1997. Kerry spends months precisely quilting close grids onto the backgrounds of her quilts, grids which then throw the other quilting motifs into relief.

ANDREW PAYNE

A phenomenon of the late-twentieth-century quilt revival has been the creation of art quilts. These are quilts which, from their inception, seek to venture beyond the domestic environment, and are made to be hung or sold in an art gallery or an exhibition which emphasises their artistic qualities. This is in contrast with quilts from the past which generally began in domesticity, and although some have latterly been given the status of art and hung in museums, art galleries and corporate spaces, this was never part of the maker's intention These art quilts are usually called 'contemporary' quilts or 'innovative' quilts, even though both these names are not altogether adequate as, taken literally, all quilts created in the present could be called contemporary, and originality of design may be found in quilts which look traditional. However, usage has given the word 'contemporary' its meaning when it is used in this context.

ANDREW PAYNE

ANDREW PAYNE

QUILT MADE BY EARLWOOD PIECEMAKERS *(top)*,
'Blanket of Love'. 55 cm x 55 cm (22 in x 22in).
QUILT MADE BY EARLWOOD PIECEMAKERS *(above)*,
'Blanket of Love'. 60 cm x 60 cm (24 in x 24 in).
QUILT PANEL MADE BY BRIAN EARL *(far right).*

Some artists came into quilting from other disciplines because they found in quilting an expressive medium, and also because there were organised exhibitions in which their work could be shown. Many quilters moved from making traditional quilts into making art quilts as their skills, vision and experience grew. Quilts were represented in other broader fibre Exhibitions, such as the Tamworth Fibre/Textile Festival. The promotion of quilt exhibitions in art galleries was given a boost in 1991 when the Manly Art Gallery, Sydney, began a series of quilt exhibitions titled 'The New Quilt'.

Judy Hooworth has been a quilter involved with these exhibitions, both in the organising and in showing her quilts. Originally trained in art, she became an art teacher after leaving art school. Judy was self-taught in quiltmaking, and joined a small local group of women who got together to quilt in the 1970s. Later she was active in organised quilting during the 1980s. Judy uses strong vibrant colours in her mainly-pieced quilts, and is particularly known for her love of yellow, which to her is 'the colour of life and energy'. Judy is also one of the small number of Australian quilters whose work has been selected for the prestigious biennial Quilt National exhibition in the United States. In 1993, her quilt 'Composition in Yellow' was chosen. The quilt has Log Cabin pieced blocks in red and yellow which vibrate against sashing of jagged black and white. Judy combines both hand- and machine-quilting in her work.

The long tradition of making quilts for charity and good causes continued with enthusiasm. Local schools and hospitals, children's charities and churches, nursing homes and hospices, museums and service clubs, the unique Australian Flying Doctor Service, big charities such as the Red Cross, and even Mother Theresa's work in India, have all benefited from quilts. Some charity quilts were made to raise funds through raffles, and many thousands of dollars were collected because quilts are valued as prizes. For instance, in 1997 the Canberra Quilters made and raffled a blue scrap quilt to raise money for the Neonatal Intensive Care Unit of the Canberra Hospital. Other charity quilts were made to be given away. The Earlwood Piecemakers group, of Sydney, make quilts for the Neonatal Intensive Care Unit of the King George V Hospital. They call the quilts 'Blankets of Love'. The work was instigated by Shirley Zions, who understood the special sorrow parents have for babies who die before or soon after birth – tiny lives snuffed out before they have begun. The little quilts, made from simple patterns and pretty bright colours, are wrapped around the baby when the parents and family say farewell. It may be the only time some of the parents have held their baby. The family may keep the little quilt as a keepsake which can offer some small solace in their sorrow and help in their recovery.

Australians participated in the worldwide movement to make quilts as memorials for those who died from HIV/AIDS, and the Quilt Project was begun in Sydney in 1988. The Quilt was made up of panels made by friends or family of someone who had died, and each panel contained personally significant images or messages. Again, a quilt helped with mourning, both through the process of making and through the finished panel which became a memorial when assembled into the larger whole. The Quilt was displayed, in parts or altogether, in all states and territories of Australia, making a sober and loving testimony to the lives lost. Brian Earl made a panel for Stuart Challender, the conductor of the Sydney Symphony Orchestra, who died in 1991. Brian sewed the quilt panel for Stuart's friend, Wendy, who did not sew. On the panel he appliquéd 'Der Rosenkavalier' (the last opera Stuart Challender conducted), and also appliquéd a silver rose, to represent the one in the opera that was later given to Stuart.

Another aspect of quiltmaking in the 1980s and 1990s was the creation of quilts for public spaces.

ANDREW PAYNE

These quilts, usually group efforts, celebrated local places and their history. Groups in towns as diversely situated as Narrabri in New South Wales to Kalgoorlie in Western Australia worked on quilted wallhangings which were then hung in public buildings. The Camden Country Quilters made a quilt for the Camden Council, to celebrate the area's bicentenary. It was named the 'Cowpastures Heritage Quilt' because the Camden area was originally called Cowpastures after a herd of cattle was discovered there in 1795. The cattle had escaped from the First Fleet, and had multiplied after finding the good pastures near the Nepean river, south-west of Sydney. It was also the area where John Macarthur took up a large grant of land, naming his property Camden Park. Good grazing land, it also had coal and silver deposits, fertile soil for market gardens and vineyards, and timber. All this history, the beauty of the landscape, and the

diversity of flora and fauna, are depicted on the quilt. The quilt, which today hangs in the Camden Civic Centre, was unveiled in February 1995 by the then Governor of New South Wales, Rear Admiral Peter Sinclair.

During the 1980s and 1990s, Australian women embraced quiltmaking as never before, making thousands of quilts in all kinds of styles and all kinds of fabrics, and with all levels of skill. Women could

find their own niche in quilting, from the occasional maker to the professional, from making small things to making large bed quilts, from following traditions to making contemporary art quilts. Australian women made quiltmaking their own.

QUILT MADE BY CAMDEN COUNTRY QUILTERS *(above)*, *'Cowpastures Heritage Quilt', 1995. 242 cm x 242 cm (95 in x 95 in). Collection of Camden Council, New South Wales.*